Measuring the Performance of Human Service Programs

SAGE HUMAN SERVICES GUIDES

A series of books edited by ARMAND LAUFFER and CHARLES D. GARVIN. Published in cooperation with the University of Michigan School of Social Work and other organizations.

1: **GRANTSMANSHIP** by Armand Lauffer (second edition)
2: **CREATING GROUPS** by Harvey J. Bertcher and Frank M. Maple (second edition)
10: **GROUP PARTICIPATION** by Harvey J. Bertcher (second edition)
11: **BE ASSERTIVE** by Sandra Stone Sundel and Martin Sundel
14: **NEEDS ASSESSMENT** by Keith A. Neuber with William T. Atkins, James A. Jacobson, and Nicholas A. Reuterman
15: **DEVELOPING CASEWORK SKILLS** by James A. Pippin
17: **EFFECTIVE MEETINGS** by John E. Tropman (second edition)
20: **CHANGING ORGANIZATIONS AND COMMUNITY PROGRAMS** by Jack Rothman, John L. Erlich, and Joseph G. Teresa
25: **HELPING WOMEN COPE WITH GRIEF** by Phyllis R. Silverman
29: **EVALUATING YOUR AGENCY'S PROGRAMS** by Michael J. Austin, Gary Cox, Naomi Gottlieb, J. David Hawkins, Jean M. Kruzich, and Ronald Rauch
30: **ASSESSMENT TOOLS** by Armand Lauffer
31: **UNDERSTANDING PROGRAM EVALUATION** by Leonard Rutman and George Mowbray
33: **FAMILY ASSESSMENT** by Adele M. Holman
35: **SUPERVISION** by Eileen Gambrill and Theodore J. Stein
37: **STRESS MANAGEMENT FOR HUMAN SERVICES** by Richard E. Farmer, Lynn Hunt Monohan, and Reinhold W. Hekeler
38: **FAMILY CAREGIVERS AND DEPENDENT ELDERLY** by Dianne Springer and Timothy H. Brubaker
39: **DESIGNING AND IMPLEMENTING PROCEDURES FOR HEALTH AND HUMAN SERVICES** by Morris Schaefer
40: **GROUP THERAPY WITH ALCOHOLICS** by Baruch Levine and Virginia Gallogly
41: **DYNAMIC INTERVIEWING** by Frank F. Maple
43: **CAREERS, COLLEAGUES, AND CONFLICTS** by Armand Lauffer
45: **TREATING ANXIETY DISORDERS** by Bruce A. Thyer
46: **TREATING ALCOHOLISM** by Norman K. Denzin
47: **WORKING UNDER THE SAFETY NET** by Steve Burghardt and Michael Fabricant
48: **MANAGING HUMAN SERVICES PERSONNEL** by Peter J. Pecora and Michael J. Austin

49: **IMPLEMENTING CHANGE IN SERVICE PROGRAMS** by Morris Schaefer
50: **PLANNING FOR RESEARCH** by Raymond M. Berger and Michael A. Patchner
51: **IMPLEMENTING THE RESEARCH PLAN** by Raymond M. Berger and Michael A. Patchner
52: **MANAGING CONFLICT** by Herb Bisno
53: **STRATEGIES FOR HELPING VICTIMS OF ELDER MISTREATMENT** by Risa S. Breckman and Ronald D. Adelman
54: **COMPUTERIZING YOUR AGENCY'S INFORMATION SYSTEM** by Denise E. Bronson, Donald C. Pelz, and Eileen Trzcinski
55: **HOW PERSONAL GROWTH AND TASK GROUPS WORK** by Robert K. Conyne
56: **COMMUNICATION BASICS FOR HUMAN SERVICE PROFESSIONALS** by Elam Nunnally and Caryl Moy
57: **COMMUNICATION DISORDERS IN AGING** edited by Raymond H. Hull and Kathleen M. Griffin
58: **THE PRACTICE OF CASE MANAGEMENT** by David P. Moxley
59: **MEASUREMENT IN DIRECT PRACTICE** by Betty J. Blythe and Tony Tripodi
60: **BUILDING COALITIONS IN THE HUMAN SERVICES** by Milan J. Dluhy with the assistance of Sanford L. Kravitz
61: **PSYCHIATRIC MEDICATIONS** by Kenneth J. Bender
62: **PRACTICE WISDOM** by Donald F. Krill
63: **PROPOSAL WRITING** by Soraya M. Coley and Cynthia A. Scheinberg
64: **QUALITY ASSURANCE FOR LONG-TERM CARE PROVIDERS** by William Ammentorp, Kenneth D. Gossett, and Nancy Euchner Poe
65: **GROUP COUNSELING WITH JUVENILE DELINQUENTS** by Matthew L. Ferrara
66: **ADVANCED CASE MANAGEMENT: NEW STRATEGIES FOR THE NINETIES** by Norma Radol Raiff and Barbara Shore
67: **TOTAL QUALITY MANAGEMENT IN HUMAN SERVICE ORGANIZATIONS** by Lawrence L. Martin
68: **CONDUCTING NEEDS ASSESSMENTS** by Fernando I. Soriano
69: **ORAL HISTORY IN SOCIAL WORK** by Ruth R. Martin
71: **MEASURING THE PERFORMANCE OF HUMAN SERVICE PROGRAMS** by Lawrence L. Martin and Peter M. Kettner

Measuring the Performance of Human Service Programs

Lawrence L. Martin
Peter M. Kettner

SHSG SAGE HUMAN SERVICES GUIDES 71

*Published in cooperation with the University
of Michigan School of Social Work*

SAGE Publications
International Educational and Professional Publisher
Thousand Oaks   London   New Delhi

For information address:

SAGE Publications, Inc.
2455 Teller Road
Thousand Oaks, California 91320
E-mail: order@sagepub.com

SAGE Publications Ltd.
6 Bonhill Street
London EC2A 4PU
United Kingdom

SAGE Publications India Pvt. Ltd.
M-32 Market
Greater Kailash I
New Delhi 110 048 India

Printed in the United States of America

Library of Congress Cataloging-in-Publication Data

Martin, Lawrence L.
   Measuring the performance of human service programs / authors,
Lawrence L. Martin, Peter M. Kettner.
      p. cm. —(Sage human services guides; v. 71)
   Includes bibliographical references and index.
   ISBN 0-8039-7134-6 (cloth: acid-free paper). —ISBN 0-8039-7135-4
(pbk.: acid-free paper)
      1. Human services—Evaluation—Methodology. 2. Evaluation
research (Social action programs) 3. Client outcomes.
I. Kettner, Peter M., 1936- . II. Title. III. Series.
HV11.M3494   1996
362'.068'4—dc20   95-41794

This book is printed on acid-free paper

                99 00 10 9 8 7 6 5 4

Sage Production Editor: Gillian Dickens

CONTENTS

Preface   xi

1. Performance Measurement: The New Accountability   1

   Introduction   1
   What Is Performance Measurement?   3
   Performance Measurement and the Systems Model   3
   The Efficiency Perspective   4
   The Quality Perspective   5
   The Effectiveness Perspective   6
   Why Adopt Performance Measurement?   8
   Performance Measurement and Improving
      Program Management   8
   Performance Measurement and Resource Allocations   9
   Performance Measurement as a Forced Choice   10

2. Performance Measurement: An Idea Whose Time Has Come   11

   Introduction   11
   Forces Promoting Performance Measurement   11
   Government Performance and Results Act   12
   National Performance Review   12
   Total Quality Management Approach   13
   Managed Care   13
   Service Efforts and Accomplishments Reporting   14
   Language and Structure of SEA Reporting   15
   Service Efforts   15
   Service Accomplishments   16

Service Efforts and Accomplishments Ratios	17
Adopting the Language and Structure of SEA Reporting	18
Developing and Using Performance Measures	19
3. Social Problems, Human Service Programs, and Performance Measurement	20
Introduction	20
Determining the Number of Human Service Programs	22
Specifying the Social Problem	23
Identifying the Assumptions	24
The Social Problem of Drugs	25
The Social Problem of Homelessness	26
The Social Problem of Educational Underachievement of Disadvantaged Children	27
4. Output Performance Measures	31
Introduction	31
What Are Output Performance Measures?	31
Developing Intermediate Output Performance Measures	33
Definition of Unit of Service	33
Types of Units of Service	33
Selecting a Unit of Service	35
Units of Service and Programs of Services	36
Final Output Performance Measures	37
Defining a Service Completion	37
Developing Service Completions	38
Service Completions and Client Outcomes	39
5. Quality Performance Measures	41
Introduction	41
What Is Quality?	41
Types of Quality Performance Measures	44
Outputs With Quality Dimensions Approach	45
Client Satisfaction Approach	47
6. Outcome Performance Measures	50
Introduction	50
What Are Outcome Performance Measures?	50
Client Problems Versus Client End States	51
The Four Types of Outcome Performance Measures	51
Intermediate and Ultimate Outcome Performance Measures	53

Selecting Outcome Performance Measures 54
Cause-and-Effect Relationships 55
Social Indicators as Ultimate Outcome
    Performance Measures 56
Outcome Performance Measures and
    Programs of Services 58
Assessing the Four Types of Outcome
    Performance Measures 60

7. Numeric Counts 62

Introduction 62
What Are Numeric Counts? 62
Examples of Numeric Counts 63
The Florida Department of Health and
    Rehabilitative Services 65
The Preference for Numeric Counts 67
An Assessment of Numeric Counts 68

8. Standardized Measures 71

Introduction 71
What Are Standardized Measures? 71
Types of Standardized Measures 74
    Substantive Focus 74
    Who Completes Them? 74
    Response Scales 76
Using Standardized Measures as Outcome
    Performance Measures 76
Translating Standardized Measures Into Numeric Counts 77
An Assessment of Standardized Measures 78
Resources for Use in Selecting Standardized Measures 79
    Sources of Selected Clinical Standardized Measures 79
    Sources of Selected Standardized Measures
        for Services to Families and Children 80
    Sources of Selected Standardized Measures
        for Employment-Related Services 81
    Sources of Selected Standardized Measures for
        Services to Older Persons 82

9. Level of Functioning Scales 84

Introduction 84
What Are LOF Scales? 84

Principles in Designing LOF Scales   86
  Developing a Conceptual Framework   86
  Developing Descriptors   86
  Respondent Considerations   89
  Constructing LOF Scales   90
  A Case Example: LOF Scales in a Child
    Residential Treatment Center   92
  Translating LOF Scales Into Numeric Counts   94
  An Assessment of LOF Scales   94

10. Client Satisfaction   96

  Introduction   96
  Using Client Satisfaction as an Outcome
    Performance Measure   96
  Translating Client Satisfaction Outcomes
    Into Numeric Counts   97
  An Assessment of Client Satisfaction   98
  An Assessment of the Four Types of
    Outcome Performance Measures   99

11. Issues in Selecting, Collecting, Reporting, and
    Using Performance Measures   101

  Introduction   101
  Issues in Selecting Performance Measures   101
    Failing to Relate Performance Measures
      to Program Mission   102
    Relying Too Heavily on Existing Data   102
    Excluding Stakeholders From the Process   102
    Selecting Too Few Quality Performance Measures   102
  Issues in Reporting Performance Measurement Data   103
    The Frequency of Performance Measurement Reporting   103
    The Cost of Collecting Performance Measurement Data   103
    The Displaying of Performance Measurement Data   104
  Issues in Using Performance Measurement Data   106
    Improving Direct Delivery   106
    Improving Contract Delivery   108
  Does Performance Measurement Really Make a Difference?   109
  Conclusion   110

Appendix A: New Beginnings Residential Treatment
  Center Case Study   111

Appendix B: Answers to Exercises From New
    Beginnings Residential Treatment Center Case Study   118

References   125

Index   129

About the Authors   139

PREFACE

One of the more important influences shaping human service programs today is the renewed emphasis on accountability and performance measurement. Perhaps at no other time in recent history have human service programs been under more pressure from stakeholders to demonstrate their efficiency, their quality, and their effectiveness. This book provides an introduction to the concepts and tools of performance measurement.

We wish to recognize and thank some colleagues for their contributions to the bibliography of standardized measures that appears in Chapter 8: Dr. Steven L. McMurtry of the School of Social Work at Arizona State University, for his assistance with standardized measures for services for families and children; Dr. Ann Nichols-Casebolt of the School of Social Work at Virginia Commonwealth University, for her assistance with standardized measures for employment-related services; and Dr. F. Ellen Netting, also of the School of Social Work at Virginia Commonwealth University, for her assistance with standardized measures for services for older persons.

We also wish to thank Dr. Armand Lauffer of the School of Social Work at the University of Michigan, who guided us in the preparation of this book.

—LAWRENCE L. MARTIN
—PETER M. KETTNER

Chapter 1

PERFORMANCE MEASUREMENT
The New Accountability

INTRODUCTION

For the foreseeable future, human service programs will be characterized by two themes: a lack of resources and a lack of stakeholder confidence. The magnitude of the federal budget deficit, combined with the conservative mood of Congress, almost precludes any consideration of new federal funding for human service programs (Connors, 1991). Many federal human service programs may find themselves transformed into block grants, reduced in funding, and turned over to the states. The ability of the states to make up for federal funding cuts is problematic. Forty-seven of 48 states responding to a recent survey indicated they were operating in a cutback management mode (Drucker & Robinson, 1993).

The lack of federal and state resources is felt not only by government human service programs but by programs operated by many private nonprofit and for-profit organizations as well. Government human service programs are *directly* affected because they rely on federal and state appropriations for the overwhelming portion of their revenues. Human service programs operated by private nonprofit and for-profit organizations are *indirectly* affected because of their widespread dependency on purchase of service contracts (Kettner & Martin, 1994; Kramer, 1994). When government appropriations for human service programs get cut, purchase of service contracts also gets cut.

The human services also suffer from a crisis of confidence. Congress and the administration both are taking hard looks at many human service programs. Leaders of some of the largest states, including California and

TABLE 1.1 Human Service Program Stakeholders

- Clients
- Citizens
- Elected officials
- Advocacy groups
- Government funding agencies
- Foundations
- Board members
- Agency administrators
- Accountants and auditors
- Others

New York, have made similar statements. For the present, at least, the desire to scrutinize human service programs appears related more to a general dissatisfaction with their *performance* rather than to any generalized repudiation of their intrinsic or moral worth.

The renewed concern with the performance of human service programs is not unexpected, nor is it a particularly new phenomenon. Government has historically reacted to periods of fiscal stress and budget deficits by placing an increased emphasis on program performance and accountability—not just for human service programs but for all programs funded with public tax dollars (Netting, Kettner, & McMurtry, 1993). Government in the 1990s appears to be simply following tradition.

A major task confronting human service programs today is to demonstrate to stakeholders that they work. As Table 1.1 illustrates, the term *stakeholder* is used broadly to include clients, citizens, elected officials, advocacy groups, government funding agencies, foundations, board members, agency administrators, accountants and auditors, and any other group that is affected by, or has an interest in, a particular human service program.

The old arguments that human service programs deal with soft services and complex "messy" social problems that defy performance specification and measurement are no longer acceptable to many stakeholders. In fact, Carter (1983) suggested that this argument became unacceptable to stakeholders some time ago. If Carter was right, then the failure of human service programs to demonstrate their efficacy during the 1980s may partially explain the situation they find themselves in today. The key to human service programs demonstrating their efficacy and winning back the support of their stakeholders may well lie in the concept of performance accountability and in the tools of performance measurement.

WHAT IS PERFORMANCE MEASUREMENT?

Performance measurement can be defined as the regular collection and reporting of information about the efficiency, quality, and effectiveness of human service programs (Urban Institute, 1980). For example, in a foster care program, performance measurement would be concerned with the regular collection and reporting of such information as the amount of service provided by the program, the quality of that service, the results or impacts of the program, and the costs involved measured in both dollars and personnel.

Performance measurement is only one of many optional approaches to program accountability. Other approaches include process accountability, fiscal accountability, legal accountability, service delivery accountability, and others (Rossi & Freeman, 1993). What makes performance measurement different, and important for human service programs, is its increasing popularity with government agencies at the federal, state, and local levels. Performance measurement's popularity may be due to its comprehensive nature. Performance measurement combines three major accountability perspectives into one:

1. the efficiency perspective,
2. the quality perspective, and
3. the effectiveness perspective.

This multifaceted approach enables performance information on human service programs to be viewed from different perspectives by different stakeholders holding different opinions about the nature of accountability (Boschken, 1994; Rossi & Freeman, 1993). Performance measurement implies no hierarchy or preference among these three perspectives but rather assumes that all three perspectives are important to at least some stakeholders.

PERFORMANCE MEASUREMENT
AND THE SYSTEMS MODEL

In discussing performance and performance measurement, it is useful to refer to the systems model. The systems model has long been used as an aid in understanding how human service programs operate (e.g., Ables & Murphy, 1981; Kettner, Moroney, & Martin, 1990; Rosenberg & Brody, 1974). As Figure 1.1 illustrates, the core elements of the systems model are inputs, process, outputs, and feedback:

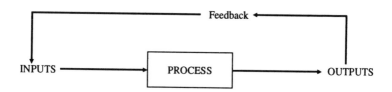

Figure 1.1. The Systems Model

- *Inputs* are anything a system (or a human service program) uses to accomplish its purposes (Swiss, 1991). More specifically, inputs can be thought of as the resources and raw materials (e.g., funding, staff, facilities, equipment, clients, presenting problems, etc.) that go into a human service program (Kettner et al., 1990).
- *Process* constitutes the actual treatment or service delivery (i.e., the human service program) during which inputs are consumed and translated into outputs (Churchman, 1968).
- *Outputs* are anything a system, or a human service program, produces (Swiss, 1991).
- *Feedback* can be thought of as information about the performance of a system, or a human service program, that is reintroduced into the system as an input.

The system elements of inputs, outputs, and feedback are used to explain the three accountability perspectives of efficiency, quality, and effectiveness.

THE EFFICIENCY PERSPECTIVE

Performance measurement includes a focus on efficiency accountability. From this perspective (see Figure 1.2), the primary performance measure for a human service program is a comparison of outputs and inputs. For example, in looking at a human service program from the efficiency perspective, one assesses the amount of service provided and the numbers of clients completing the program (outputs) and compares these measures against the costs involved (inputs).

The ratio of outputs to inputs is the classical definition of productivity (Brinkerhoff & Dressler, 1990). Accordingly, feedback on the performance of a human service program, as Figure 1.2 illustrates, takes the form of tracking and reporting on outputs. An accountable human service program, according to the efficiency perspective, is one that strives to maximize outputs in relation to inputs.

The efficiency approach to accountability has never been popular in human service programs (Pruger & Miller, 1991). All too frequently, efficien-

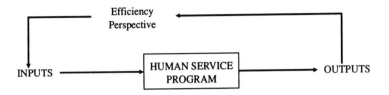

Figure 1.2. The Systems Model and the Efficiency Perspective

cy has been used as a rationale for funding cuts and—in some instances—for outright attacks on the legitimacy of human service programs (Knapp, 1991). Many human service administrators view a focus on efficiency accountability as misguided, all too frequently resulting in goal displacement. "You can do the wrong thing very efficiently" is a criticism frequently vocalized. Conversely, the perception held by some stakeholders (e.g., citizens, voters, elected officials, and some foundations) is that only 10 cents of every human service program dollar actually get "to people who need help"; the remainder, they believe, is lost because of inefficiency (Swiss, 1991, p. 14).

Despite the criticisms made of efficiency in the past, several good reasons exist why it should be a major accountability focus of human service programs in the 1990s and beyond. First, the requirements of public stewardship demand that every dollar spent on human service programs be put to the best possible use to ensure that every eligible client is served and that every client served receives the best available and affordable service. Second, efficiency or productivity considerations are a basic operating assumption of most fee-for-service contracts and managed care programs. Finally, a high-profile position supporting efficiency or productivity is necessary to counter the image held by some stakeholders that human service programs waste taxpayer and contributor dollars.

THE QUALITY PERSPECTIVE

A focus on service quality accountability differs from the efficiency perspective. Service quality accountability is an essential component of the total quality management (TQM) movement. Throughout the 1980s, the writings of the major quality management gurus—such as Crosby (1980, 1985), Deming (1986), Feigenbaum (1983), and Juran (1988, 1989)—have had a major impact on management thinking and practices in the United States. Government programs, including those defined as human service, are now frequently required to assess the quality of their services and to "benchmark"—or compare their results—with other programs operated by

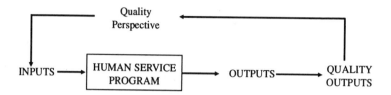

Figure 1.3. The Expanded Systems Model and the Quality Perspective

both public and private agencies (Spendolini, 1992). In general, government programs have not fared well in this benchmarking process. According to one recent survey, government services were ranked dead last in quality behind banking, airlines, and auto repair shops (Swiss, 1991).

The TQM movement has reworked the classical definition of productivity to include quality considerations. According to TQM theory, productivity is increased when programs provide high-quality services and is decreased when low-quality services are provided. For human service programs, the implication of this expanded definition of productivity is that high-quality services should result in lower error rates, less paperwork, less processing time, happier funding sources, more satisfied clients, lower costs, and a better public image. Thus, there appears to be more than a mere connection between a focus on quality accountability and a focus on efficiency accountability.

TQM goes beyond the old conceptualization of productivity as simply the ratio of outputs to inputs. As shown in Figure 1.3, TQM extends the systems model to focus on quality as the primary measure of performance and changes the definition of productivity to the ratio of *outputs that meet a specified quality standard* to inputs (Martin, 1993)—for example, the proportion of meals in a home-delivered meals program that arrive hot or the proportion of riders in a specialized transportation program who are picked up on time.

Feedback on the performance of human service programs necessarily takes the form of tracking and reporting on quality (see Figure 1.3). An accountable human service program according to the quality perspective is one that strives to maximize quality outputs in relation to inputs.

THE EFFECTIVENESS PERSPECTIVE

From the effectiveness perspective, performance measurement incorporates a focus on outcomes (i.e., the results, impacts, and accomplishments) of human service programs (Epstein, 1992). Examples include the number of children who are placed for adoption by an adoptions program,

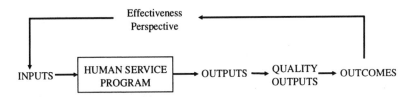

Figure 1.4. The Expanded Systems Model and the Effectiveness Perspective

the number of parents who stop abusing and neglecting their children as the result of a parent skills training program, and the number of juvenile offenders who have no further encounters with the juvenile justice system as a result of an intensive case management program.

Effectiveness is regularly advanced as the highest form of performance accountability in human service programs (Patti, 1987; Pruger & Miller, 1991). Effectiveness considerations have also been added to some definitions of productivity (Brinkerhoff & Dressler, 1990).

Unlike traditional program evaluation, performance measurement is not concerned with one-shot assessments of results, accomplishments, or impact. Instead, performance measurement belongs to the school of thought that holds that human service programs cannot be divorced from their social settings (Cronbach, 1982). Consequently, performance measurement is less concerned with attempting to demonstrate scientifically defensible cause-and-effect relationships (Rocheleau, 1988) and is more concerned with basic practice questions, such as what outcomes are achieved by what types of human service programs (Wholey & Hatry, 1992). Performance measurement enables judgments to be made about the effectiveness of human service programs during implementation as well as after, thus capturing both the formative and summative approaches to evaluation.

The effectiveness perspective on accountability again extends the language of the systems model. As Figure 1.4 demonstrates, effectiveness accountability is concerned with the ratio of outcomes to inputs. Accordingly, feedback on the performance of human service programs takes the form of tracking and reporting on outcomes. An accountable human service program, according to the effectiveness perspective, is one that strives to maximize outcomes in relation to inputs.

When Figures 1.2, 1.3, and 1.4 are compared, it is apparent that the efficiency, quality, and effectiveness perspectives to human service program accountability are distinctive. Not only do the three perspectives conceptualize program performance accountability differently, but also they emphasize different types of feedback. Because performance measurement

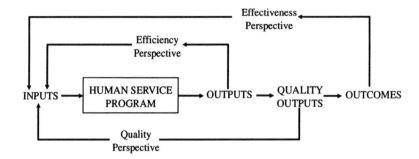

Figure 1.5. The Expanded Systems Model and Performance Measurement

draws on all three perspectives, it creates one comprehensive approach to accountability (see Figure 1.5).

WHY ADOPT PERFORMANCE MEASUREMENT?

Why should human service administrators adopt performance measurement? In addition to accountability reporting, are there other important factors to consider? Proponents of performance measurement point out at least three:

1. Performance measurement has the potential to improve the management of human service programs.
2. Performance measurement has the potential to affect the allocation of resources to human service programs.
3. Perhaps most important, performance measurement may be a forced choice for many, if not most, human service programs.

PERFORMANCE MEASUREMENT
AND IMPROVING PROGRAM MANAGEMENT

To properly manage their human service programs, administrators must be clear about the following questions:

- Who are their clients?
- What are their demographic characteristics?
- What are their social or presenting problems?
- What services are they receiving?
- In what amounts?

- What is the level of service quality?
- What results are being achieved?
- At what costs?

Most human service programs are relatively clear about the answers to the first four questions, some are frequently unclear about the latter four, and still others are not even sure what the questions are. For the most part, the inability of human service programs to answer all eight questions is largely because of the absence of formally adopted measures of output, quality, and outcome.

Performance measurement provides the missing piece that can enable administrators to answer all eight questions about their human service programs. Combining performance measurement data with client and problem data provides administrators with the ability to identify which human service programs achieve what results with what types of clients and at what costs. Armed with this type of information, human service administrators should be able to plan, design, and implement more efficient, more effective, and better quality programs.

If the above arguments are not sufficient, performance measurement has still other features to recommend it as a valuable management tool for human service administrators. As will be demonstrated, performance measurement:

1. promotes "client centeredness" by making client outcomes a central component of agency performance (Poertner & Rapp, 1987, p. 23),
2. provides a common language that human service administrators can use to make evaluative judgments about the efficiency, quality, and effectiveness of the programs they manage (Brinkerhoff & Dressler, 1990),
3. enables human service administrators to continually monitor their programs to identify "points of intervention" for service improvements (Poertner & Rapp, 1985, p. 65), and
4. improves the morale of direct service workers who get feedback on what clients are being helped and by how much (Carter, 1983).

PERFORMANCE MEASUREMENT
AND RESOURCE ALLOCATIONS

Performance measurement also has the potential to significantly affect government and nongovernment resource allocation decisions to human service programs. If all human service programs were to collect and report comparable performance measures, then government and private funding sources could use the resulting information to make budgeting, grant, and contracting decisions.

What is the purpose, some might ask, of collecting information on the performance of human service programs, if the data are not then used to reward those that perform and to penalize those that do not? For example, take two private voluntary family service agencies (Agency X and Agency Y), both operating in the same community and both receiving the majority of their funding from the United Way. Agency X provides more service (outputs) and gets better results with clients (outcomes) for less money than Agency Y. In an era of downsizing and budget reductions, Agency X is going to be considerably more attractive to the United Way than is Agency Y. Performance measurement, then, has the potential to significantly affect not only the politics of the human service budgetary process (Wildvasky, 1974) but also the politics of human service funding in general—and, perhaps, the overall politics of government budgeting and funding as well. The adoption of performance measurement is not restricted to human service programs. All government programs are candidates for performance measurement. Consequently, performance measurement—carried to its logical conclusion—could become an important factor not only in making resource allocation decisions between competing human service programs but also in making resource allocation decisions between the human services and other competing societal needs including health care, housing, infrastructure, and others.

PERFORMANCE MEASUREMENT
AS A FORCED CHOICE

Although some administrators might prefer to ignore the opportunity to adopt performance measures, they may have little choice in the matter. Forces already under way may ultimately determine that many, if not most, human service programs will be required to implement performance measurement sometime during the decade of the 1990s. The forces promoting performance measurement and the implications of these forces for human service programs are discussed in Chapter 2.

Chapter 2

PERFORMANCE MEASUREMENT
An Idea Whose Time Has Come

INTRODUCTION

The federal government, as well as many state and some local governments, is currently taking steps to make performance measurement an integral part of its basic management systems—not just for human service programs but for all publicly funded programs. At the federal level, performance measurement is destined to become increasingly important, irrespective of which political party controls the White House or the Congress and regardless of whether most federal programs remain categorical in nature or are turned over to the states as block grants. Because of the influence on the human service system exerted by federal and state funds, most human service programs—be they government or private sector—can expect eventually to become involved with performance measurement.

FORCES PROMOTING
PERFORMANCE MEASUREMENT

Five major forces promoting performance measurement in government —and by extension in the human services—can be identified. Individually, each of these forces is important by itself. Combined, they virtually ensure that every human service program will eventually be required to develop, use, and report performance measures. These five major forces are:

1. the Government Performance and Results Act of 1993,
2. the National Performance Review,

3. the total quality management (TQM) approach,
4. managed care, and
5. the service efforts and accomplishments (SEA) reporting initiative of the Governmental Accounting Standards Board (GASB).

GOVERNMENT PERFORMANCE AND RESULTS ACT

In 1993, the U.S. Congress passed the Government Performance and Results Act. Passed into law with strong Democratic and Republican support, this act specifies that beginning with fiscal year 1998, all federal departments must begin reporting on effectiveness (outcome) performance measures (Gore, 1993). In the past, federal departments such as Health and Human Services (HHS), Housing and Urban Development (HUD), and the Department of Labor (DOL) have tended to pass along their congressional mandates to their grantees and contractors. Consequently, it is likely that public and private human service programs receiving funding from HHS, HUD, and DOL will eventually be required to collect and report data on outcome performance measures. Without collecting at least some outcome data from the actual providers of services, it is unclear how the requirements of the Government Performance and Results Act can be satisfied. Some 75 pilot projects under this act are already under way in HHS, HUD, and DOL and in some 27 other federal departments (Hatry & Wholey, 1994; Rosenbloom, 1995). In addition, many of the block grant proposals made by both the White House and the Congress include performance measurement requirements (Federal Office of Management and Budget [FOMB], 1995; "Power to the States," 1995).

NATIONAL PERFORMANCE REVIEW

One of the more important books currently influencing government practices is *Reinventing Government* (Osborn & Gaebler, 1992). These authors devote an entire chapter to the topic of results-oriented government, including the use of performance measurement. Osborn and Gaebler argue convincingly that "what gets measured gets done" (p. 146).

The National Performance Review is the name given to the federal government's efforts to implement the principles contained in *Reinventing Government,* including an emphasis on performance measurement. One of the major goals of the National Performance Review is to speed up implementation of the Government Performance and Results Act (1993). The National Performance Review calls for full implementation of this act by the fall of 1997. At this time, all federal departments are to submit plans for the tracking and reporting of performance measures with specific emphasis on outcomes (FOMB, 1995; Gore, 1993). The FOMB plans to present Congress with the first annual "Government Wide Performance Plan" as part of the fiscal year 1998 budget (FOMB, 1995, p. 137).

Again, it is reasonable to assume that federal departments such as HHS, HUD, and DOL will require their government and private sector grantees and contractors to collect and report information on performance measures with special emphasis on outcomes. Without the participation of grantees and contractors, little information will exist to be reported.

TOTAL QUALITY MANAGEMENT APPROACH

TQM is both a response to, and a force promoting, performance measurement. In addition to making administrators more conscious about promoting quality in their human service programs, the TQM movement has also affected the nature of performance measurement itself.

Quality performance measures now routinely take their place alongside more traditional efficiency and effectiveness performance measures (Brinkerhoff & Dressler, 1990; Martin, 1993). Quality performance measures generally take one of two forms: (a) consumer (client) satisfaction and (b) outputs related to some quality standard. An example of the first approach is the proportion of clients in a specialized transportation program who rate the quality of the service as either *very good* or *excellent*. Examples of the second approach include (a) the proportion of meals in a home-delivered meals program that arrive hot and (b) the proportion of graduates in a federally funded Job Training Partnership Act program who possess marketable job skills on completion of training.

The development, collection, and interpretation of quality performance measures pose a major challenge for human service programs. Because quality management is relatively new to the human services, little literature exists to guide practice.

MANAGED CARE

Managed care is a collective term used to describe a variety of ideas about health care delivery (Cornelius, 1994). Although managed care is primarily a health service phenomenon, it does affect the human services in the areas of drugs, alcohol, and mental health. In addition to the goal of promoting efficiency by switching from fee-for-service to prepaid capitation funding relationships, managed care programs are also forcing provider agencies to become more concerned with outcome performance measurement (Austin, Blum, & Murtaza, 1995).

A focus on outcome performance measurement is a critical aspect of managed care programs regardless of the status (public or private) of the payer. For example,

• The state of California, long known as a "bellwether" state, has totally restructured its public mental health delivery system to provide client-centered services using outcome performance measures (Austin et al., 1995, p. 205).

• The Managed Mental Healthcare Association, a group of some 150 major corporations, has created an Outcomes Management Consortium that is developing standardized disorder-specific outcome performance measures (England & Goff, 1993, p. 5).

SERVICE EFFORTS AND
ACCOMPLISHMENTS REPORTING

For many years now, the Governmental Accounting Standards Board (GASB) has set financial accounting and reporting standards for state and local governments. The standards established by GASB become what are known as "generally accepted accounting principles" for state and local governments (Fountain & Robb, 1994, p. 12). For state and local governments to receive "unqualified opinions" (i.e., no exceptions noted) on their financial reports from certified public accountants and auditors, all GASB standards must be met (Epstein, 1992, p. 513; Fountain & Robb, 1994, p. 12).

For the past several years, GASB has been experimenting with the idea of going beyond accounting and financial reporting and also requiring state and local government to engage in what it calls service efforts and accomplishments reporting (Epstein, 1992; GASB, 1993, 1994). *SEA reporting is simply GASB's term for performance measurement.* Epstein (1992) estimates that SEA reporting will become a reality before the year 2000.

The significance of SEA reporting for the human services is considerable—perhaps the most powerful and far-reaching of the five major forces discussed here. When SEA reporting becomes mandatory, all state and local government agencies, including human service agencies, will be required to participate in the collection and reporting of performance measures. Those private nonprofit and for-profit human service agencies that hold grants or contracts from state or local governments will also be affected. The only way state and local governments can collect and report performance measures on the totality of their human service programs is to require their private nonprofit and for-profit grantees and contractors to also participate and report.

Together, the Government Performance and Results Act, the National Performance Review, the TQM movement, managed care, and SEA reporting are likely to require the adoption of performance measurement for many, if not most, human service programs. Any questions about this conclusion will probably be concerned more with *when* rather than with *if.*

LANGUAGE AND
STRUCTURE OF SEA REPORTING

SEA reporting is arguably the most important of the five major forces promoting increased accountability and the use of performance measurement. SEA reporting represents a systematic approach to performance measurement with an identifiable structure and language. The other four major forces promoting performance measurement lack the specificity and guidance provided by SEA reporting. SEA reporting is compatible with the others, however. For this reason, SEA reporting could well subsume the others. The result would be a single approach common to all government-funded programs (human services and non-human services), regardless of the implementing agency: federal government, state government, local government, private nonprofit, or private for-profit.

Because of the importance of SEA reporting for performance measurement in general, and the human services in particular, this book adopts its language and structure throughout. SEA reporting is based on the expanded systems model that includes (a) inputs, (b) outputs, (c) quality outputs, and (d) outcomes—but excludes process. The absence of the process component is consistent with SEA's primary focus: performance and performance cost considerations.

SEA reporting can be divided into three elements. As Table 2.1 illustrates, these are (a) service efforts, (b) service accomplishments, and (c) measures, or ratios, that relate service efforts to service accomplishments (GASB, 1994).

SERVICE EFFORTS

Service efforts are the resources (inputs) that go into a human service program. The GASB measures service efforts in three primary ways: (a) the total cost of the program, (b) the total full-time equivalent (FTE) positions devoted to the program, and (c) the total number of employee hours worked on the program. It should be noted that SEA reporting assumes that agencies operating multiple human service programs have already adopted, or have the capability to adopt, program budgeting. The importance of this assumption should not be overlooked. The performance cost ratios (i.e., cost per output and cost per outcome) cannot be determined if an agency has not defined its program structure and/or lacks a method for allocating organizational costs to the identified programs. Table 2.2 is designed to reflect the fiscal year reporting of service efforts for a family counseling program providing intensive training and counseling to abusive and/or neglecting parents.

TABLE 2.1 The Elements of Service Efforts and Accomplishments Reporting

I. Service Efforts
A. Financial information
  1. Total cost measured in dollars
B. Nonfinancial information
  1. Number of personnel: the total number of full-time equivalent (FTE) positions
  2. Other measures (e.g., the total number of employee hours expended)

II. Service Accomplishments
A. Outputs
  1. Total volume of service provided
  2. Proportion (%) of the total service volume that meets a specified quality standard
B. Outcomes
  1. Measures of the results, accomplishments, or impacts achieved (partially or totally)

III. Service Efforts and Accomplishments Ratios
A. Efficiency measures
  1. The ratio of service volume (outputs) to resources consumed (inputs) as measured by
    a. Cost per output
    b. Outputs per FTE
    c. Outputs per hour worked
B. Effectiveness measures
  1. The ratio of results, accomplishments, or impacts (outcomes) to resources consumed (inputs) as measured by
    a. Cost per outcome
    b. Outcomes per FTE
    c. Outcomes per hour worked

SERVICE ACCOMPLISHMENTS

Service accomplishments are divided into two main categories: (a) *outputs* and (b) *outcomes* (which capture the effectiveness perspective on accountability). Outputs are further subdivided into (a) *outputs* (which capture the efficiency perspective of accountability) and (b) *outputs that meet a specified quality standard* (which capture the quality perspective of accountability). The GASB (1994) is concerned with establishing standards of performance reporting and not with establishing standards of performance:

> The mission of GASB is to establish standards of accounting and financial reporting that will provide useful information and will guide and educate the public. This mission limits the Board's [GASB] focus to establishing standards for the *reporting of information about performance as distinct from establishing standards of performance*. Establishing performance standards is beyond the scope of the GASB. (p. 1)

TABLE 2.2 Service Efforts and Accomplishments Input Elements

Service Efforts	Example
1. Total cost	$750,000
2. FTEs	22
3. Hours worked	45,760*

NOTE: *Based on a 2,080-hour (52 weeks × 40 hours per week) work year for 22 employees.

TABLE 2.3 Service Efforts and Accomplishments Output and Outcome Elements

Service Accomplishments	Example
1. Outputs	
a. The quantity of service provided measured in units of service	27,500 hours of parent training and counseling provided
b. The quantity of service provided measured in service completions*	225 parents complete the program
c. The quantity of service provided that meets a specified quality standard	At least 85% of completing parents ($n = 191$) rate the service as *very helpful* or *helpful*
2. Outcomes	At least 50% of completing parents ($n = 112$) will have no reports of abuse or neglect for a minimum of 2 years following treatment

NOTE: *A service completion equals one client completing treatment or receiving a full complement of services.

The GASB is saying essentially that the determination of performance-reporting categories (outputs, outputs with quality dimensions, and outcomes) is within its purview but that the selection of specific output, output with quality dimensions, and outcome performance measures for human service programs is not. Administrators of human service programs will be expected to develop their own performance measures or adopt those developed by other programs or agencies. Table 2.3 presents some potential fiscal year service accomplishments for the sample family counseling program.

SERVICE EFFORTS AND ACCOMPLISHMENTS RATIOS

SEA ratios are the third element in SEA reporting. These ratios relate service efforts to service accomplishments through such measures as

TABLE 2.4 Service Efforts and Accomplishments Ratios

SEA Ratios	Example
1. Efficiency (Output) Measures	
a. Cost per unit of service	$27.27 ($750,000 ÷ 27,500)
b. Units of service per FTE	1,250 (27,500 ÷ 22)
c. Cost per service completion	$3,333 ($750,000 ÷ 225)
d. Service completions per FTE	10.3 (225 ÷ 22)
2. Effectiveness (Outcome) Measures	
a. Cost per unit of outcome	$6,696 ($750,000 ÷ 112)
b. Outcomes per FTE	5.1 (112 ÷ 22)

3. Interpretations

1.a.	The average cost per hour of training is $27.27.
1.b.	Each trainer provided an average of 1,250 hours of training.
1.c.	The average cost per family completing the training is $3,333.
1.d.	Each trainer resulted in an average of 10.3 families completing the training.
2.a.	The cost to achieve the outcome of one family not abusing or neglecting its children for a minimum period of 2 years is $6,696.
2.b.	The average number of outcomes attributable to each trainer is 5.1.

1. cost per unit of service (output or outcome),

2. units of service per FTE, and

3. units of service per hour worked.

Table 2.4 presents some examples of what SEA ratios might look like for the sample family counseling program. As can be seen, the SEA ratios provide a variety of ways of assessing accountability in the family counseling agency. There is something for just about every conceivable human service stakeholder group. Some measures may be of more interest to citizens, elected officials, and advocacy groups; others to government funding agencies, accountants, and auditors; and still others to clients, board members, and agency administrators.

ADOPTING THE LANGUAGE
AND STRUCTURE OF SEA REPORTING

Many state and local government human service programs and agencies are already moving ahead with performance measurement by adopting the language and structure of SEA reporting. For example, the states of Connecticut, Oregon, Minnesota, and Virginia are currently engaged in widespread experimentation with the use of SEA reporting (Craymer & Hawkins, 1993; Epstein, 1992). Local governments are also experimenting with SEA reporting, including Phoenix, Sunnyvale (California), Milwaukee, New York City, and Palm Beach County in Florida (Fountain & Robb, 1994).

TABLE 2.5 An Overview of Performance Measures

Output Performance Measures		Outcome Performance Measures	
Intermediate	*Final*	*Intermediate*	*Ultimate*
Episode or contact	Service	Numeric counts	Numeric counts
unit of service	completions		
Material unit		Standardized	Standardized
of service		measures	measures
		Level of	Level of
		functioning scales	functioning scales
Time unit of service		Client satisfaction	
	Quality Performance Measures		
	Outputs with quality dimensions		
	Client satisfaction		

DEVELOPING AND USING
PERFORMANCE MEASURES

In subsequent chapters, the development and use of performance measures based on the SEA reporting format are discussed in depth, including outputs, outputs with quality dimensions, and outcomes. Table 2.5 provides an overview of the categories and types of performance measures to be discussed.

As Table 2.5 illustrates, the discussion of output performance measures is organized around two broad categories, intermediate outputs and final outputs. Intermediate outputs use episode, material, and time unit of service measures. Final outputs use a measure called a *service completion*. The discussion of quality performance measures involves two types of measures, output measures with quality dimensions and client satisfaction. The discussion of outcome performance measures is organized around two broad categories (intermediate outcomes and ultimate outcomes) and four distinct types: numeric counts, standardized measures, level of functioning scales, and client satisfaction. These classifications and terms are defined and discussed in detail in subsequent chapters.

Before dealing with the actual development and use of performance measures, a discussion about the relationship between social problems, human service programs, and the selection of performance measures is in order. This discussion is the subject of Chapter 3.

Chapter 3

SOCIAL PROBLEMS, HUMAN SERVICE PROGRAMS, AND PERFORMANCE MEASUREMENT

INTRODUCTION

A relationship should exist between the performance measures selected for use in human service programs and the social problems that particular human service programs address. To illustrate, homeless shelter programs exist to address the social problem of homelessness; congregate meals programs for older persons exist to address the social problem of poor nutrition and social isolation among older persons; and job training programs exist to address the social problem of unemployment. If this point seems self-evident, consider for a moment the types of measures that human service programs have historically used to describe what they do:

- The number of clients served
- The number of unduplicated clients served
- The amount of funding expended

These so-called performance measures really say nothing about performance, let alone anything about the social problem a program is supposed to address.

Because human service programs exist to address social problems, performance measures in general—and outcome performance measures more specifically—should provide information relative to social problems. For example, performance measures for homeless shelter programs should provide information about what the programs are doing to address and

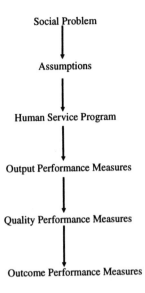

Social Problem

↓

Assumptions

↓

Human Service Program

↓

Output Performance Measures

↓

Quality Performance Measures

↓

Outcome Performance Measures

Figure 3.1. The Link Between Performance Measures, Programs, and Social Problems

alleviate homelessness. Performance measures for congregate meals programs for older persons should provide information about what the programs are doing to address and alleviate inadequate nutrition and social isolation among older persons. Job training programs should provide information about what the programs are doing to address and alleviate the social problem of unemployment.

This chapter deals with the relationship between performance measures, human service programs, and social problems. We suggest that all human service programs be subjected to a program analysis prior to the actual development of performance measures. Program analysis consists of three major tasks:

Task 1: Determining how many human service programs an organization has

Task 2: Specifying the social problem each human service program addresses

Task 3: Identifying the assumptions each human service program makes about the social problem it addresses

Program analysis makes explicit the linkages among social problems, human service programs, and performance measures. As Figure 3.1 suggests, when the three major tasks of program analysis are accomplished, the actual development of output, quality, and outcome performance measures become tasks in a series of interconnected activities. In turn, the performance measures provide accountability information (feedback) about what human service programs are doing to address or alleviate the identified social problems.

DETERMINING THE NUMBER
OF HUMAN SERVICE PROGRAMS

The first task of program analysis is determining how many human service programs an organization has. In general, a program can be defined as "a prearranged set of activities which specify the means to achieve a goal. In the public sector (health, education, welfare, and government), a program is formulated in order to provide services which accomplish defined objectives" (Delbeck, Van de Ven, & Gustafson, 1975, pp. 1-2).

A more concise definition of a program is offered by Starling (1993): "a major organizational endeavor with an objective" (p. 16). If these two definitions are collapsed and if the requirement that human service programs should address social problems is added, then four criteria describing a human service program can be derived. A human service program:

1. addresses an identified social problem,
2. represents a significant proportion of the total activity of an organization,
3. has goals and objectives (either formally stated or implied), and
4. has designated resources, including personnel (because no activity or endeavor can take place without resources).

These four criteria—and particularly the first criterion—rule out administrative activities such as personnel, finance, facilities management, clerical pool, and the like from being considered human service programs.

Beyond the guidance provided by these criteria, the determination of exactly how many human service programs an organization has is really more art than science. Anthony and Young (1994), however, suggest that no organization should have more than 10 programs. The rationale for this cutoff point is that with more than 10 programs, an organization has too many competing priorities (too many goals and objectives) that undermine the chances of any one program being successful.

The identification of how many human service programs an organization has is necessary because performance measurement uses *program* as its unit of analysis. SEA reporting has formally adopted programs as the unit of analysis and requires that all performance measures data (both programmatic and financial) be reported by programs. Preliminary results of pilot projects implemented under the Government Performance and Results Act (1993) indicate that the program is also frequently designated as the unit of analysis (Hatry & Wholey, 1994). Any output, quality, or outcome performance measures developed for human service programs with the expectation of satisfying either SEA reporting or the Government Performance and Results Act should be based on—or be capable of being aggregated to—the level of individual human service programs.

Other reasons also exist for making programs the unit of analysis for performance measurement. For example, many important stakeholders of human service programs (e.g., elected officials, government funding agencies, and foundations) tend to think of, and to fund, programs. In addition, a canon of the accounting profession, another important stakeholder, is that all government and nonprofit organizations exist for the primary purpose of carrying out programs (Anthony & Young, 1994).

An additional implication of making programs the unit of analysis for performance measurement is that all human service organizations will necessarily have to adopt program budgeting. Program budgeting requires that all costs (both direct and indirect) of operating an organization be allocated to its various programs (Anthony & Young, 1994; Lynch, 1985). The adoption of program budgeting is necessary to develop the cost per output and cost per outcome ratios required by SEA reporting. An in-depth discussion of program budgeting is beyond the scope of this book, but any basic text on budgeting and financial management for nonprofit organizations (e.g., Anthony & Young, 1994; Lynch, 1985) should provide an adequate treatment of the subject.

SPECIFYING THE SOCIAL PROBLEM

After an organization has identified how many human service programs it has, the second task of program analysis is to specify the social problem (e.g., unemployment, homelessness, crime, child abuse and neglect, teenage pregnancy, mental illness, etc.) that each program addresses. For many human service programs, specifying the social problem is a relatively straightforward proposition. In some instances, however, the social problem may have to be inferred.

Most human service programs are created to address a specific social problem. They are generally funded through categorical grants and contracts and include such programs as Head Start, WIN, job training, and food stamps. For human service programs of this type, the language of the law, statute, or ordinance creating the program or its implementing regulations generally specifies the social problem. If these sources are silent, the social problem can still be identified by a reading of federal or state legislative digests or the transcripts of committee hearings and meetings to get a "sense" of the program.

Some federal funding sources are designed to address social problems and social welfare needs from a broader perspective. These federal funding sources are not linked to any particular social problem and are more like "funding streams" than they are like human service programs. An example is the Social Services Block Grant (SSBG). The SSBG, as well as most other human service block grants, funds a variety of human service programs dealing with a variety of social problems. For federal funding sources, or funding streams, of this type, the specified social problem cannot be determined by consulting some law, statute, ordinance, or regulation but must be inferred from the nature of the human service program itself. For example, if SSBG funding is used to support a child abuse prevention program, then the social problem the program addresses is child abuse. Likewise, if SSBG funding is used to support a community mental health clinic, then the social problem the program addresses is community mental health. Human service programs such as SSBG actually wind up addressing many different social problems. If recent proposals at the federal level about transforming many categorical federal programs into block grants come to pass, more human service programs at the state and local levels may find themselves in the position of having to infer the social problems they address rather than finding any explicit statement in federal law or regulation.

Regardless of how the connection is made, it is important for the development of useful performance measures that the link between human service programs and specified social problems be made. After this connection is made, the third step in program analysis is to determine the assumptions that human service programs make about the causes of the social problems they address.

IDENTIFYING THE ASSUMPTIONS

Human service programs are also based on assumptions about the causes of social problems. Social problems tend to be multifaceted. Social problems such as unemployment, poverty, crime, drugs, and others have multiple causes, not just one. On the other hand, human service programs frequently deal with only one cause of a social problem. Unfortunately, the underlying assumptions that human service programs make about the causes of social problems are frequently left unstated. Even when the social problem that a human service program addresses is explicitly stated in law, statute, or ordinance, the assumptions made about the cause of the social problem may go unstated. The challenge for performance measurement— to say nothing of the challenge of developing better human service programs —is that different assumptions about the cause of a social problem may call for different programs and different performance measures.

The process of identifying the assumptions that human service programs make about social problems is again likely to be more art than science. Few, if any, formal guidelines exist. Support for assumptions can be drawn from the human service literature on the subject, including theoretical frameworks and models, current research, evaluation studies, and practice experience. The following three examples are designed to demonstrate how the assumptions that human service programs make about the causes of the social problems they address can affect the selection of performance measures. The first example deals with the social problem of drugs; the second with the social problem of homelessness; the third with the social problem of the educational underachievement of children who are disadvantaged.

THE SOCIAL PROBLEM OF DRUGS

This example involves two human service programs designed to address the social problem of drugs; each is based on a different assumption about the cause of the social problem. The result is an entirely different set of output, quality, and outcome performance measures. The first program provides drug abuse education; the second program provides drug abuse counseling and rehabilitation. The first program is based on the assumption that the social problem of drugs is because of a lack of knowledge and information; if more people are educated about the dangers of drugs, they will not use drugs and the social problem of drugs will decrease. The second program is based on the assumption that the social problem of drugs is a result of underlying mental and/or emotional problems that manifest themselves in drug abuse; if more current drug abusers can get counseling to deal with their mental and/or emotional problems, the number of existing drug abusers will decline and the social problem of drugs will decrease.

Is one of these assumptions about the cause of the social problem of drugs more correct than the other? Perhaps, perhaps not. Differing assumptions about the cause of the social problem of drugs can lead to different human service programs and, ultimately, to the selection of different sets of performance measures. As Figure 3.2 illustrates, the performance measures (output, quality, and outcome) that would be most useful in reporting performance accountability information to the stakeholders of a drug abuse education program are probably different from those that would be most useful to the stakeholders of a drug abuse counseling and rehabilitation program.

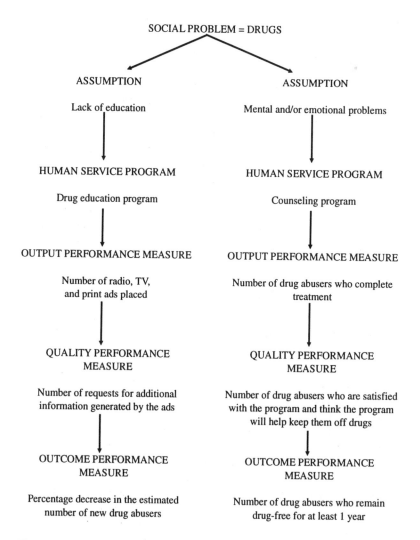

Figure 3.2. Performance Measures for Two Human Service Programs Addressing the Social Problem of Drugs

THE SOCIAL PROBLEM OF HOMELESSNESS

In the following example, two human service programs designed to address the social problem of homelessness are considered. Again, each program is based on differing assumptions about the cause of the social problem of homelessness. The first program provides short-term emergency shelter for individuals and families. The unstated assumption is that homelessness results from episodic problems of individuals and families who have lost their jobs or who have been evicted and are temporarily homeless until they find work or move in with family or friends. The second program provides long-term shelter and a comprehensive program of services including basic education, money and debt management, job training, drug abuse counseling and rehabilitation, and others. The unstated assumption here is that homelessness results from chronic problems of individuals and families who have deep-seated and long-standing problems that require prolonged treatment. Which assumption about the cause of the social problem of homelessness is most accurate? They both are; homelessness—like drug abuse—is again a multifaceted social problem.

In this example (see Figure 3.3), the most useful outcome performance measure for providing accountability information to stakeholders about what the two programs are doing to address and alleviate homelessness is probably the number of individuals and families who cease to be homeless. Likewise, the most useful quality performance measure for both programs might well be some measure of client satisfaction. But when it comes to output performance measures, the two programs might well diverge. A useful performance measure for the first program dealing with episodic homelessness might be simply the number of shelter care days of service. For the second program dealing with chronic homelessness, it might be more useful to develop a series of output performance measures that capture information about the various service components of the program (i.e., job training, basic education, drug counseling and rehabilitation, etc.).

The first program dealing with episodic homelessness should clearly produce more outcomes than the second, which deals with chronic homelessness, because clients will spend more time in the second program than in the first. It would be decidedly unfair to make comparisons between these two programs using these same performance measures, but this is a problem in interpreting performance measures, not in developing them.

THE SOCIAL PROBLEM OF EDUCATIONAL UNDERACHIEVEMENT OF DISADVANTAGED CHILDREN

The third example demonstrates how different assumptions made about the causes of a social problem can even result in different components of the same human service program requiring different types of performance measures. This example deals with an actual situation dating to the early 1980s when we attempted to develop performance measures for a Head Start program operating in Maricopa County (Phoenix), Arizona. The Maricopa

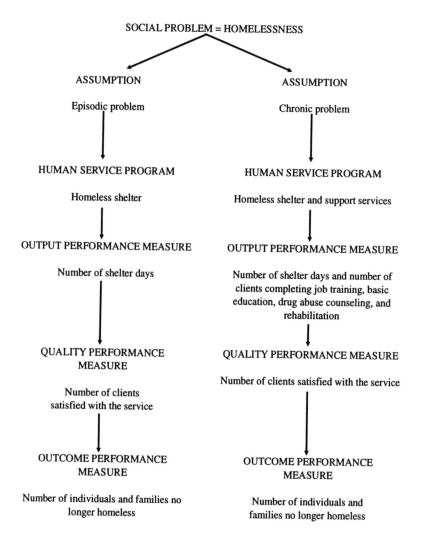

Figure 3.3. Performance Measures for Two Human Service Programs Addressing the Social Problem of Homelessness

County Head Start program actually consisted of two human service programs. The first program could be called "traditional Head Start"; the second program could be called "home base." Both of these human service programs were directed at a common social problem (educational underachievement of children who were disadvantaged), but they were based on different assumptions about cause.

The traditional Head Start program assumed that educational underachievement resulted from the inability of low-income families to afford or access quality preschool education. The home base program was predicated on the assumption that educational underachievement resulted because families did not value education or appreciate the connection between educational achievement and good nutrition, the maintenance of good health, and parenting skills. During the attempt to develop performance measures for the two component programs, it became apparent that for the traditional Head Start program, the most useful performance measures would be those that provided accountability information about individual children, whereas in the case of the home base program, the most useful performance measures would be those that provided accountability information about families. The suggested performance measures are shown in Figure 3.4. Each of the two outcome performance measures shown did, of course, require additional refinement for measurement purposes. Quality performance measures were not developed because at the time, the importance of quality in programs was still waiting to be discovered.

These examples illustrate the importance of linking human service programs to identified social problems and specifying the assumptions that human service programs make about the causes of the social problems that they address. In Chapter 4, the discussion turns to the development of performance measures, beginning with output performance measures.

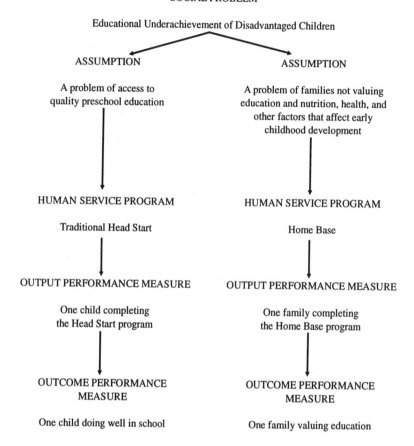

Figure 3.4. Performance Measures for Two Components of the Same Human Service Program

Chapter 4

OUTPUT PERFORMANCE MEASURES

INTRODUCTION

Anyone who has ever operated a small business knows how important output performance measures are. Restaurant operators count the number of meals they serve. Service station operators count the number of gallons of gasoline they pump. Taxi operators count the number of trips their vehicles make. These output performance measures provide feedback to the business operators on how well they are doing in the amount of service provided or the amount of product sold. When outputs and output performance measures are compared with inputs (the costs of doing business), the resulting productivity ratio is a measure of the business's relative efficiency. Outputs and output performance measures serve the same function in human service programs.

WHAT ARE OUTPUT PERFORMANCE MEASURES?

Outputs can be broadly defined as anything that a system (or a human service program) produces (Swiss, 1991). Output performance measures capture information about the type and amount of outputs produced by a system.

As Table 4.1 illustrates, systems and, by extension, human service programs, produce two types of outputs (intermediate and final) and thus have the need for two types of output performance measures (Brinkerhoff & Dressler, 1990). Final outputs are the end products of a system or a human service program. Intermediate outputs are the products and services consumed in the production of final outputs. In human service programs, final

TABLE 4.1 Types of Output Performance Measures

1. Intermediate Outputs
    The products and services produced and consumed in production of final outputs
2. Final Outputs
    The end products of a human service program

TABLE 4.2 Types of Output Performance Measures for Human Service Programs

Intermediate Outputs	Final Outputs
Units of service	Service completions

outputs and final output performance measures have a *client focus;* intermediate outputs and intermediate output performance measures have a *service focus.* The following example of an adoption program should help in clarifying why both types of output performance measures are important in human service programs.

An adoption program can be said to engage in two activities: (a) the placement of children with adoptive parents and (b) the screening and assessment of prospective adoptive parents. The final output, or end product, of the adoption program is one child adopted. The intermediate output, or the measure of services and/or products consumed in the generation of one final output, is the number of screening and assessment visits made. If the program makes five screening and assessment visits with a prospective adoptive family and subsequently places a child with that family, the program has produced one final output and five intermediate outputs.

If the adoption program were to keep track only of the number of children adopted, the amount of activity (intermediate outputs) actually required to accomplish the end result would go unaccounted for. Conversely, if the adoption program were to keep track only of the number of screening and assessment visits made, the actual number of adoptions (final outputs) generated by all this activity would go unaccounted for. When combined, however, the intermediate and final output performance measures provide a comprehensive picture of the adoption program.

Intermediate output and final output performance measures are not new concepts to the human services. As Table 4.2 illustrates, intermediate output performance measures are also known as *units of service* (Bowers & Bowers, 1976; Kettner et al., 1990), whereas final output performance measures are also known as *service completions* (Ables & Murphy, 1981; Kettner & Martin, 1993).

TABLE 4.3 Three Types of Units of Service

Service	Unit of Service
Information and referral	One contact or one referral (contact or episode)
Home-delivered meals	One meal (material)
Counseling services	One hour (time)

DEVELOPING INTERMEDIATE
OUTPUT PERFORMANCE MEASURES

Most administrators of human service programs are probably familiar with units of service. The term *unit of service* has been around at least since the early 1970s. During this period, a study of the use of intermediate output performance measures in state purchase of service contracting was commissioned by the then federal Department of Health, Education, and Welfare. The results were published in a final report titled *The Elusive Unit of Service* (Bowers & Bowers, 1976). The term stuck and joined the human services lexicon as another name for an intermediate output performance measure.

DEFINITION OF UNIT OF SERVICE

A unit of service is a standardized measure used to determine and report how much service is provided by a human service program. In other words, a unit of service is a program-specific measure of service volume. The human services encompass a wide variety of programs. Day care (both child and adult), counseling, parent training, recreation, job training, and others all fall into the category of human services; all need, and can benefit from, measures of service volume. For this reason, different types of units of service or intermediate output performance measures have been developed.

TYPES OF UNITS OF SERVICE

Units of service are measured in three different ways: (a) an episode or contact unit, (b) a material unit, and (c) a time unit (Bowers & Bowers, 1976; Kettner & Martin, 1993).

Table 4.3 provides examples of these three types of units of service using three common human service programs (information and referral, home-delivered meals, and counseling).

An episode or contact unit of service is defined as one contact between a worker and a client. It is used when the recording of client contact information is important but when the actual duration (time) of the contact is not considered important.

A material unit of service is a tangible resource provided to a client and can include such items as a meal, a food basket, articles of clothing, cash, a prescription, and so forth. Material units are generally considered to be the least precise of the three types of units of service because of the variation that can exist between individual units. For example, the number of items in two food baskets can vary widely, but each basket is still counted as one unit of service.

A time unit can be expressed in minutes, hours, days, weeks, or months, depending on the needs of individual human service programs. A time unit is generally considered the most precise of the three types of units of service because it is expressed in standardized increments. When time is used as a unit of service, it is important to state whether the time only refers to direct client contact time or if support activity time (e.g., completing paperwork, attending client staffings, etc.) is also included. Different time units also have different cost implications that may not be readily apparent at first. The selection of a time unit of service for child day care services in the state of Arizona provides a case example.

Developing a Unit of Service for Child Day Care Services

In the late 1970s, the state of Arizona decided to make child day care services readily available to welfare clients. This goal was to be accomplished by contracting with privately operated child day care centers. For contracting as well as reporting purposes, a unit of service for child day care services was needed. A statewide task force was created to recommend an appropriate unit of service. The task force included state welfare department employees, child day care center operators, and other stakeholders.

The child day care center operators wanted the unit of service to be 1 day, regardless of whether a child was in care for only 1 hour or a full 8 hours. The state welfare department employees wanted to use 1 hour as the unit of service so that the state would be paying for only the amount of time a child was actually in care. The child day care center operators argued that using 1 hour as the unit of service was cumbersome and would create needless paperwork. The unit of service finally agreed on was 1 day, but 1 day was further defined as anything more than 4.5 hours of care. Any lesser amount of care was not to be considered as a unit of service and was not to be reported or billed.

SELECTING A UNIT OF SERVICE

Selecting a unit of service for a particular human service program involves a three-step process.

Step 1

Convene a focus group or committee that is broadly representative of the stakeholders involved in the particular human service program.

Step 2

Brainstorm different units of service including episode or contact units, material units, and time units. This approach frequently leads to the identification of potentially more useful units of service than might otherwise be the case. The group members might consult existing human service taxonomies that have been developed by some states. These taxonomies generally contain suggested units of service. A sample of some suggested units of service taken from the *Arizona Taxonomy of Human Services* (Arizona Department of Economic Security [ADES], 1988) is shown in an appendix at the end of this chapter.

Step 3

Evaluate each suggested unit of service according to the following five criteria: utility, precision, feasibility, unit cost reporting, and consensus.

1. *Utility:* This criterion refers to the extent to which the information generated is considered useful and relevant (Millar & Millar, 1981). Utility has meaning only in relation to stakeholders (Nurius & Hudson, 1993). As discussed in Chapter 3, the most useful unit of service is the one that provides the most relevant information to stakeholders about a human service program given the nature of the social problem the program addresses and the assumptions made about the social problem. Usefulness is probably the most important criterion of the five listed here (Wholey & Hatry, 1992).

2. *Precision:* As a general rule, the more precise the unit of service, the more precise the information generated about human services programs. The need for precision in units of service must be balanced, however, against the third criterion.

3. *Feasibility:* The feasibility criterion refers to the time and effort required by program staff to collect and report unit of service data. For

TABLE 4.4 A Quarterly Report on Adult Day Care Units of Service

Adult Day Care Service	1,000 days
Service components	
1. Transportation component	1,900 trips
2. Meals component	900 meals
3. Socialization and recreation component	5,200 hours
4. Health screening component	200 screenings

example, using 15 minutes as a time unit of service as opposed to 1 hour means that program staff must collect and report four times as many data. In the same vein, if a homeless shelter makes used clothing available to residents, collecting data using a material unit of service (one item of clothing) requires more time and effort than collecting data using a contact unit of service (one resident visiting the clothing center).

4. *Unit cost reporting:* Unit costs (how much it costs to provide one unit of service) are used for a variety of purposes in human service programs, including computing break-even points; forecasting revenues, expenses, and caseloads; and purchasing of service contracting. The relative ability of different units of service to generate needed unit cost data may influence the selection of a particular type.

5. *Consensus:* Stakeholders of a human service program reach agreement that they will collect, report, use, and respect the unit of service agreed on. A unit of service represents a common language that all operators of a particular human service program agree to speak.

UNITS OF SERVICE AND PROGRAMS OF SERVICES

Some human service programs are composed of multiple services. A good example is adult day care. Adult day care programs can include a transportation component, a congregate meals component, a socialization and recreation component, a health component, and others. A unit of service for adult day care might be based on a time unit—1 day, for example. On the basis of this time unit of service, if each of 20 seniors participates in the program five times during a week, the adult day care program would generate 100 units of service, or intermediate outputs, for the week. But this unit of service (1 day) does not actually say much about what the adult day care program really does.

Table 4.4 illustrates how a unit of service, or intermediate output performance measure, report might appear for an adult day care program when the various service components are separately identified and reported. A more comprehensive, meaningful, and powerful picture emerges. Now units of service, or intermediate output performance measures, are used not just for accountability purposes but also as a communications device. An additional benefit of using units of service in this manner is that the adult day care center administrator now has considerably more data about the program that can be used for planning and budgeting purposes.

FINAL OUTPUT PERFORMANCE MEASURES

A business can be relatively efficient or productive as measured by the number of customers who frequent the business (a contact unit of service) but relatively inefficient or unproductive if these customers purchase little. Likewise, a human service program can be relatively efficient or productive in providing a high volume of service as measured by units of service, or intermediate output performance measures, but relatively inefficient or unproductive if few clients complete the treatment process. In human service programs in which dropout rates are high, the results that are achieved tend to be costly. As various stakeholders (including citizens, elected officials, and government funding agencies) increasingly ask questions about completion rates, human service programs need to be able to provide efficiency or productivity accountability information about final output performance measures or service completions.

DEFINING A SERVICE COMPLETION

A service completion, or a final output performance measure, can be defined as one client completing treatment or receiving a full complement of services (Ables & Murphy, 1981; Kettner & Martin, 1993; Kettner et al., 1990). The concept of a service completion has been used in the field of medicine for a long time but is not as widely used in human service programs. In the practice of medicine, a physician may prescribe a particular medication that a patient is supposed to take for 10 days because this length of time is considered necessary for the treatment to effect a cure. Consequently, if the patient stops taking the medication after 5 days, no expectation should exist that a cure will be effected. By analogy, if a client of a human service program does not complete treatment or does not receive a full complement of services, no expectation should exist that the treatment will be effective. Take the case of a parenting skills training program for abusive and neglecting parents. If the training program consists of 10 sessions, and if all 10 sessions are considered essential to altering abusive and neglecting behavior, then it is important to know whether clients complete the full 10 sessions.

TABLE 4.5 Two Approaches to Developing Service Completions

---

1. The Standardized Approach
   a. When a minimum number of units of service (episodes, material, or time) are required for clients to complete treatment, then
   b. A service completion is one client completing treatment.
2. The Case Plan Approach
   a. When clients receive varied units of service depending on individualized needs, then
   b. A service completion is one client completing a case plan.

DEVELOPING SERVICE COMPLETIONS

As Table 4.5 illustrates, two approaches exist to determining a service completion: (a) the standardized approach and (b) the case plan approach. The selection of the appropriate approach depends on whether the treatment or service is standardized or variable.

In the standardized approach, a client must receive some minimum amount of prescribed service to complete treatment. Only at this point can a service completion report or a description of a final output be recorded. Intermediate outputs (units of service) may be of some help in determining the minimum amount of prescribed service required to complete treatment or to receive a full complement of services. For example, in human service programs that use a time unit of service (e.g., hour, day, week, and month), how many such units are required for a client to complete the program or to receive a full complement of services? The same question can be posed for human service programs that use an episode or contact unit of service. Take, for example, a group counseling program designed to assist addicts in overcoming their addictions. How many sessions are required for a client to complete the program or to receive a full complement of services? Finally, the same question can be posed for human service programs that use a material unit of service. For example, how many units of methadone must a client receive to complete the program or to receive a full complement of services?

The second approach to developing final output performance measures or service completions is the case plan approach.

Many human service programs do not have a standardized, or minimum, amount of service that clients must receive to complete treatment. For example, in a counseling program, some dysfunctional families may need 20 or 30 counseling sessions to complete treatment or to receive a full complement of services, whereas others with less severe problems may require significantly fewer sessions. Likewise, adolescents who are severely disturbed may need years of residential treatment; others may need only a short stay away from their homes. In situations such as these, it may be more useful to think of a service completion as one client completing an individual case plan. When a client has completed a case plan, a full complement of services has been provided and a service completion is recorded for the client. The case plan approach can also be applied to human service programs such as case management for persons who are chronically mentally ill or developmentally disabled, in which an expectation exists that clients will remain in treatment for extended periods. Rather than look at long-term case management services as prescribing years of treatment, services can be divided into discrete episodes lasting, for example, for 3 months. After 3 months of case management services, a client is said to have received a full complement of services and a service completion is recorded for the client.

For some human service programs, clients may enter programs with little or no expectation of exit. Examples include institutional care programs such as skilled nursing care and some long-term care alternative home-based programs. For human service programs such as these, a variant of the case plan approach can be used to determine a service completion. Although clients may be in care for extended periods with perhaps no expectation of exit, a point is nevertheless reached at which an eligibility redetermination or level of care reassessment is needed or required. The redetermination or reassessment can be treated as the break point at which the client has received a full complement of services and a service completion is recorded for the client.

SERVICE COMPLETIONS AND CLIENT OUTCOMES

In addition to serving as final output performance measures, service completions also play a role in outcome performance measurement. As a general rule, outcome performance measures should be assessed only on those *clients who complete treatment or receive a full complement of services*. This position is in keeping with the medical analogy discussed earlier in the chapter. No expectation should exist that a human service program will be effective with clients who do not complete treatment or receive a full complement of services.

The use of service completions in determining which clients should be involved in outcome performance measurement is in keeping with Rossi and Freeman's (1993) notion of a comprehensive evaluation. Rossi and Freeman make the point that one cannot draw valid conclusions about the effectiveness of a human service program if the program is not implemented as designed. Service completions distinguish between those clients who experience a human service program as it was designed and those who do

APPENDIX A Catalog of Units of Service for Selected Human Service Programs

Service	Unit
Adoption	One adoption
Advocacy services	60 minutes* of staff time
Assessment services	One assessment
Case management	60 minutes* of staff time
Counseling services	60 minutes* of staff time or one contact
Crisis hotline	One contact
Crisis intervention	One residential day** of shelter care and counseling
Disaster preparedness and relief	One case
Energy assistance	One household served
Financial assistance	One payment
Food stamps	One household served
Foster care	One calendar month of service time
Home health aide	60 minutes* of service time
Home repair/adaptation/renovation	One dwelling unit repaired, renovated, or adapted
Information and referral	One request
Interpreter services	15 minutes of staff time
Job development and placement	One placement into unsubsidized employment
Job training	One day*** of service time
Medication and medical supplies	One item
Mother and infant bonding program	One calendar month
Nursing home care	One day
Parenting skills training	60 minutes* of service time
Personal escort	One round-trip
Respite care	60 minutes* of service time, or 1 day
Shelter care and supervision	One residential day
Transportation	One trip per person, one way
Visiting nurse services	60 minutes* of service time
Weatherization	One dwelling unit weatherized

SOURCE: Arizona Department of Economic Security (1988).
NOTES: *Cumulative
**One residential day is defined as follows: If a client is receiving services on 11:59 p.m. of any day, that day is considered a full service day.
***One day is defined as 6 or more hours within a 24-hour period.

not. Some program evaluators argue that it is also important to capture evaluation data on "service noncompleters." This argument is valid but not for outcome performance measurement purposes. Data on service noncompleters may provide useful insights into the operation of human service programs and may lead to important discoveries and program improvements. Such discoveries and improvements, however, do not affect those clients who have already completed treatment or dropped out.

Chapter 5

QUALITY PERFORMANCE MEASURES

INTRODUCTION

Consider the following situation involving two eligibility workers employed in the same human service program. The first worker assesses an average of four clients per hour; the second worker assesses three clients per hour. Which worker is more productive? The efficiency perspective of accountability suggests that the first worker is. But what if the first worker makes twice as many errors as the second worker? Errors require additional staff time and resources to correct; errors can result in lost revenue due to client ineligibility. Now, which worker is more productive? The quality perspective of accountability says that the second worker is probably more productive (Crosby, 1980, 1985; Deming, 1986; Feigenbaum, 1983; Juran, 1988, 1989).

Quality performance measures are designed to keep administrators of human service programs from falling into what the quality management proponents call the "efficiency trap." Focusing on only efficiency accountability, they argue, inevitably leads to declining service quality. Declining service quality, in turn, leads to less reliable services, less timely services, more errors, more rework, increased complaints from clients and other stakeholders, more time and money spent on resolving complaints, and, in the end, lower overall productivity.

WHAT IS QUALITY?

The concept of quality is composed of a number of somewhat elusive dimensions. When people disagree about the quality of something, be it a new

41

TABLE 5.1 Some Dimensions of Quality

Dimension	Definition
Accessibility	The program is easy to access or acquire.
Assurance	Program staff are friendly, polite, considerate, and knowledgeable.
Communication	Program information is provided in simple, understandable language.
Competency	Program staff possess the requisite knowledge and skills.
Conformity	The service meets established standards.
Courtesy	Program staff demonstrate respect toward clients.
Deficiency	The program is missing a characteristic or element.
Durability	The program's performance or results do not dissipate quickly.
Empathy	Program staff attempt to understand clients' needs and provide individualized attention.
Humaneness	The program is provided in a manner that protects clients' dignity and sense of self-worth.
Performance	The program accomplishes its intended purposes.
Reliability	The program is operated in a dependable and reliable manner with minimum variation through time or between clients.
Responsiveness	The program delivery is timely.
Security	The program is provided in a safe setting free from risk or danger.
Tangibles	The appearance of the facilities, equipment, personnel, and published materials involved in program delivery is appropriate.

SOURCE: Adapted from Martin (1993).

car or a human service program, the disagreement is frequently because of different perspectives about what constitutes quality. To a great extent, quality—like beauty—lies in the eye of the beholder. Because of the relative nature of quality, a final arbiter of what constitutes quality is needed. In quality management—because of its business roots—customers are usually regarded as the final arbiters (Crosby, 1980, 1985; Deming, 1986; Juran, 1988, 1989).

Human service programs can be said to have two classes of final arbiters: (a) clients and (b) other stakeholders. Having two classes of final arbiters requires that quality performance measures incorporate the perspectives of both classes. Fortunately, performance measurement is flexible enough to accomplish this task.

Because the concept of quality is multidimensional, two initial hurdles must be overcome before quality performance measures can be developed for human service programs. The two hurdles are (a) identifying the various dimensions of quality and (b) determining which ones are most important. A recent book (Martin, 1993) dealing with total quality management in human service programs identifies some 15 generally recognized quality dimensions (see Table 5.1). With all these various quality dimensions, which ones are most important in human service programs? Recent research on service

TABLE 5.2 Five Major Quality Dimensions in Rank Order

Dimension	Weight
Reliability	32
Responsiveness	22
Assurance	19
Empathy	16
Tangibles	11

SOURCE: Adapted from Zeithaml, Parasuraman, and Berry (1990, p. 27).

quality, as well as the quality orientation of the federal government, provides some guidance in answering this question.

In a major study of service quality, researchers found a common set of quality dimensions that tend to be important to customers—and, by extension, to the clients of human service programs—regardless of the type of service (Zeithaml, Parasuraman, & Berry, 1990). In rank order and with their respective weights indicated, the preferred set of quality dimensions is shown in Table 5.2. Two quality dimensions, reliability and responsiveness, head the list.

As a quality dimension, reliability refers to how consistently the quality expectations of clients are satisfied. For example, if clients in a human service program view *assurance* and *empathy* as important quality dimensions, they will also expect consistency (reliability) in the level of assurance and empathy demonstrated by program staff from contact to contact. What does reliability mean for human service programs? Reliability means providing services in a consistent fashion; always being friendly, polite, and considerate (assurance); always attempting to understand client needs (empathy); always speaking with clients in understandable language (communication); and so forth.

When human service programs are operated in a reliable manner, clients whose quality judgments are formed on the basis of this dimension will tend to rate service quality as high. When human service programs are operated in an unreliable fashion (i.e., too much variation for no apparent reason), clients whose quality judgments are formed on the basis of this dimension will tend to rate service quality as low. How important is reliability to clients? Reliability, with its weighted score of 32 out of a possible 100 points, is considerably more important than any other quality dimension.

The second most important quality dimension is responsiveness, or timeliness. Being responsive entails providing services with a minimum of waiting. Waiting, sometimes referred to as "cycle time," is the total elapsed time between when clients need or want service and when service is actually received. Waiting, or cycle time, means not just physically waiting in some line but waiting in any and all forms (e.g., waiting for a food stamp application to be processed, for an SSI check to arrive, for a child day care voucher to be issued, for a case manager to call back, etc.). When service is provided in a responsive, or timely, fashion, clients whose quality judgments are formed on the basis of this dimension will tend to rate service quality as high.

Another view of the relative importance of the various dimensions of quality is provided by the federal government. In developing quality performance measures, federal departments—including the HHS, HUD, DOL, and others—are encouraged to create a balanced scorecard that includes quality, cycle time, and client satisfaction (Federal Accounting Standards Advisory Board [FASAB], 1994).

Apparently, the federal government views responsiveness or timeliness —or cycle time to use its words—as the most important quality dimension because it is the only one singled out for specific mention; all others are lumped together in a general category called simply "quality." The reference to client satisfaction is also interesting in that the intent is clearly to encourage federal departments to base at least some of their quality performance measures on client feedback. These two conclusions about the federal approach to quality are reinforced by the criteria used by the Federal Quality Institute (FQI) in evaluating applications from federal departments for the President's Award for Quality and Productivity Improvement. The FQI (1990) evaluation criteria single out both cycle time and client satisfaction for special mention.

What does the above discussion suggest for the development and use of quality performance measures in human service programs? First, the empirical evidence suggests that—at a minimum—human service programs should consider adopting quality performance measures that capture information about program reliability and responsiveness or timeliness. Second, human service programs—particularly those receiving federal funding— should consider basing at least some quality performance measures on client satisfaction data.

TYPES OF QUALITY
PERFORMANCE MEASURES

As Table 5.3 illustrates, two basic approaches exist to developing quality performance measures: (a) the outputs with quality dimensions approach and (b) the client satisfaction approach. These two approaches are distin-

TABLE 5.3 Two Types of Quality Performance Measures

1. Outputs With Quality Dimensions
   a. Focus: service quality
   b. Data source: agency records
2. Clients' Satisfaction
   a. Foci:
      (1) Service quality, and/or
      (2) Service results, effects, impacts, or benefits
   b. Data source: client satisfaction surveys

guished by their differing foci and their sources of quality performance measures data.

For focus, the outputs with quality dimensions approach looks exclusively at the quality of services. The client satisfaction approach, on the other hand, can look at the quality of services; at the results, impacts, or accomplishments of services; or both (Millar & Millar, 1981). For data sources, the outputs with quality dimensions approach is based on data developed from agency records; the client satisfaction approach is based on data from client satisfaction surveys.

OUTPUTS WITH QUALITY DIMENSIONS APPROACH

The outputs with quality dimensions approach involves extending intermediate output performance measures (units of service) to include quality dimensions. This process sounds a lot more complicated than it really is. A simple three-step process is all that is required. The first two steps should take into consideration the views and opinions of clients and other stakeholders and are probably best accomplished as an extension of the focus group process suggested in Chapter 4 for the development of output performance measures:

Step 1: Selecting the quality dimensions to be used
Step 2: Relating the quality dimensions to specific characteristics of human service programs
Step 3: Grafting the quality dimensions to intermediate output performance measures

Some examples will help in demonstrating and explicating each of these steps. For the sake of continuity (reliability), the three human service programs—information and referral, home-delivered meals, and counseling—used as examples of intermediate output performance measures in Chapter 4 are again used here.

Step 1: Selecting Quality Dimensions

Most human service programs will probably want—at a minimum—to select the quality dimensions of reliability and responsiveness or timeliness. The selection of other quality dimensions (e.g., assurance, competency, empathy, tangibles, etc.) will depend largely on the type of human service program and the preferences of clients and other stakeholders.

Step 2: Translating Quality Dimensions

Each quality dimension selected must be translated into a characteristic of each individual human service program. For example, what does reliability and responsiveness mean for an information and referral program, a home-delivered meals program, or a counseling program?

1. Information and referral
   a. Reliability might mean that the referrals made are appropriate (no referrals to agencies at which the caller is ineligible for service).
   b. Responsiveness might mean that callers connect on the first attempt (no busy signals).
2. Home-delivered meals
   a. Reliability might mean that meals are delivered hot (a minimum temperature of at least 180 degrees).
   b. Responsiveness might mean that meals are delivered on time (within 10 minutes of scheduled delivery time).
3. Counseling
   a. Reliability might mean that clients generally see the same counselor each time.
   b. Responsiveness or timeliness might mean that clients are not kept waiting (more than 10 minutes) for scheduled appointments.

The parenthetical comments included for each of these quality dimensions serve two purposes. First, they assist in further defining and specifying quality dimensions. Second, they also assist stakeholders in interpreting the resulting quality performance measures. Parenthetical comments such as these can be made part of the actual quality dimension itself.

Step 3: Grafting Quality Dimensions

The translated quality dimensions are grafted, or attached, to the existing intermediate output performance measures (episode, material, or time units of service) designated for the particular human service program.

TABLE 5.4 Grafting Quality Dimensions to Intermediate Output Measures (units of service)

1. Information and Referral	
a. Reliability	One appropriate referral
b. Responsiveness	One caller connecting the first time
2. Home-Delivered Meals	
a. Reliability	One meal delivered hot
b. Responsiveness	One meal delivered on time
3. Counseling	
a. Reliability	One hour of service with the counselor of record
b. Responsiveness	One hour of service when appointment started on time

In Chapter 4, the units of service designated for the three human service programs were

- Information and referral: one contact or one referral
- Home-delivered meals: one meal
- Counseling: one hour

Table 5.4 illustrates how quality dimensions might be grafted to each of these units of service.

Human service programs that use time as the unit of service or intermediate output performance measure represent something of a challenge. Experience has shown that some creativity and stretching may be necessary to make the process work. The best rule of thumb is to be guided by common sense. A quality performance measure that appears contrived may not command much respect from stakeholders and probably should be avoided. If a simple logical fit cannot be made between a quality dimension and a time unit of service, consideration should be given to either (a) selecting another unit of service, either episode or contact unit, or (b) adopting the client satisfaction approach.

CLIENT SATISFACTION APPROACH

If the outputs with quality dimensions approach to developing quality performance measures proves cumbersome, produces contrived results, or simply will not work, the client satisfaction approach can be used as an alternative. The client satisfaction approach also involves a simple three-step process with the first two steps essentially the same as for the outputs with quality dimensions approach:

Step 1: Selecting quality dimensions
Step 2: Translating the quality dimensions

In the third step, the client satisfaction approach diverges from the outputs with quality dimensions approach:

Step 3: Developing survey questions

Again, the best way to explain this three-step process is by resorting to examples. The same three human service programs (information and referral, home-delivered meals, and counseling) are again used.

Step 1: Selecting Quality Dimensions

The first step is to identify the important quality dimensions. Let us assume that client stakeholders of all three human service programs identify reliability and responsiveness or timeliness as important quality dimensions.

Step 2: Translating Quality Dimensions

Each of the two selected quality dimensions (reliability and responsiveness or timeliness) is translated into significant characteristics of each of the three human service programs. Let us assume that client stakeholders also identify the same characteristics as were used in the outputs with quality dimensions approach:

1. Information and referral
   a. Reliability: Referrals made are appropriate.
   b. Responsiveness: Callers connect on the first attempt.
2. Home-delivered meals
   a. Reliability: Meals arrive hot.
   b. Responsiveness: Meals arrive on time.
3. Counseling
   a. Reliability: Clients see the same counselor.
   b. Responsiveness: Clients are not kept waiting.

Step 3: Developing Survey Questions

A survey questionnaire is developed that includes one overall general satisfaction question and one specific question directed at each quality dimension (see Table 5.5, Part A). The purpose of the overall general satisfaction question is to allow statistics to be used to determine which quality dimensions are most important to clients. An agency with multiple

TABLE 5.5 Client Satisfaction Survey Questionnaire

A. Information and Referral

1. Overall, how satisfied are you with the information and referral program?

Very Dissatisfied				Very Satisfied
1	2	3	4	5

2. Do your contacts with the information and referral program result in referrals to agencies whose services you are eligible for?

Almost Never				Almost Always
1	2	3	4	5

3. When you call the information and referral program, do you usually get connected on the first attempt?

Almost Never				Almost Always
1	2	3	4	5

B. Home-Delivered Meals

1. Overall, how satisfied are you with the home-delivered meals program?

Very Dissatisfied				Very Satisfied
1	2	3	4	5

2. Do your home-delivered meals arrive hot?

Almost Never				Almost Always
1	2	3	4	5

3. Do your home-delivered meals arrive on time (within 10 minutes of scheduled delivery times)?

Almost Never				Almost Always
1	2	3	4	5

C. Counseling

1. Overall, how satisfied are you with the counseling program?

Very Dissatisfied				Very Satisfied
1	2	3	4	5

2. Do you see the same counselor each time you visit the agency?

Almost Never				Almost Always
1	2	3	4	5

3. Do your counseling sessions start on time (within 10 minutes of the scheduled time)?

Almost Never				Almost Always
1	2	3	4	5

human service programs would simply replicate the process for each program (see Table 5.5, Parts B and C).

In the client satisfaction approach, questions and responses must be carefully phrased. The questions and response categories shown in Table 5.5 are meant to be only examples of one approach—not the only approach or even the best approach. In addition, unless all clients are surveyed, care must be taken to ensure that a representative sample is drawn. Any basic text on survey research should provide the necessary guidance concerning question phrasing, response category development, and sampling.

Chapter 6

OUTCOME PERFORMANCE MEASURES

INTRODUCTION

Many stakeholders place a primary importance on effectiveness accountability in human service programs. Stakeholders of this persuasion argue that it is nice to know, for example, that a counseling program provided 2,000 hours of service, that 125 clients completed treatment, and that 90% of those completing treatment were either "satisfied or very satisfied" with the program. But what these stakeholders really want to know is this: What types of results, impacts, or accomplishments did the counseling program achieve?

WHAT ARE OUTCOME PERFORMANCE MEASURES?

Outcome performance measures have been broadly defined for the purposes of SEA reporting as the results or accomplishments that are attributable, at least partially, to a service or program (GASB, 1994). For purposes of human service programs, however, a more specific client focus is generally adopted. Attempts to link the outcomes of human service programs with a client focus have historically gone by such names as *client outcomes* and *client outcome monitoring*. These approaches have included assessments of client impacts and quality-of-life changes in clients as the intended outcomes of human service programs (e.g., Carter, 1983; Else, Groze, Hornby, Mirr, & Wheelock, 1992; Kettner et al., 1990; Millar, Hatry, & Koss, 1977a, 1977b; Millar & Millar, 1981; Rapp & Poertner, 1992; Schainblatt, 1977; Tatara, 1980). By blending these various themes together, we can derive the following operational definition of outcome performance measures: the results, impacts, or accomplishments of human service programs as measured by quality-of-life changes in clients.

CLIENT PROBLEMS
VERSUS CLIENT END STATES

In the human services, and particularly in social work, a tendency exists to think of clients as having problems. For example, a client may be said to have an addiction problem, a housing problem, an income problem, a child care problem, or other problems or combinations of problems. This "problem approach" is well suited to diagnosis and treatment but is less useful in thinking about the results, impacts, and accomplishments of human service programs. Telling stakeholders, for example, that 150 clients were helped with their problems may be accurate information, but it is hardly enlightening.

A more useful approach to developing outcome performance measures for human service programs is to think of anticipated, or hoped for, quality-of-life changes in clients. Quality-of-life changes can be thought of as either movement toward desirable client conditions, status, behaviors, functioning, attitudes, feelings, or perceptions or movement away from undesirable client conditions, status, behaviors, functioning, attitudes, feelings, or perceptions. This "client end state" approach has the twin advantages of emphasizing the results, impacts, and accomplishments of human service programs as well as forcing consideration about what will actually be measured (i.e., client conditions, status, behaviors, functioning, attitudes, feelings, or perceptions).

Table 6.1 provides some examples of client quality-of-life changes that might serve as outcome performance measures. Table 6.1 also demonstrates how desirable and undesirable client conditions, status, behaviors, functioning, attitudes, feelings, and perceptions are really two sides of the same coin. This dichotomy is highlighted to emphasize the point that many human service programs may already collect data on either desirable or undesirable client conditions or behaviors. These data may be capable of serving as outcome performance measures.

THE FOUR TYPES OF
OUTCOME PERFORMANCE MEASURES

Outcome performance measures can be divided into four major types. As shown in Table 6.2, these are numeric counts, standardized measures,

TABLE 6.1 Examples of Quality-of-Life Changes in Clients

1. Examples of movement toward some desirable change
   - a. Condition   A homeless client finding shelter
   - b. Status   An unemployed client getting a job
   - c. Behavior   An increase in a juvenile client's school attendance
   - d. Functioning   An increase in a client's coping skills
   - e. Attitude   An increase in a juvenile client's acceptance of the value of education
   - f. Feeling   An increase in a client's sense of belonging
   - g. Perception   An increase in a client's self-esteem
2. Examples of movement away from some undesirable change
   - a. Condition   Number of nights a homeless person spends on the streets
   - b. Status   Number of days of work missed by an employed substance-abusing client
   - c. Behavior   A decrease in the number of times a juvenile client "ditches" school
   - d. Functioning   A decrease in the incidence of a client's fighting with spouse
   - e. Attitude   A decrease in a juvenile client's number of acting-out incidents
   - f. Feeling   A decrease in a client's feeling of powerlessness over his or her environment
   - g. Perception   A decrease in a client's negative perceptions about other ethnic groups

TABLE 6.2 Four Types of Outcome Performance Measures

- Numeric counts
- Standardized measures
- Level of functioning scales
- Client satisfaction

level of functioning (LOF) scales, and client satisfaction (Kettner & Martin, 1993; Kuechler, Velasquez, & White, 1988).

Numeric counts are simple nominal counts of the numbers of clients who achieve quality-of-life changes. Standardized measures are normed before-and-after tests used to measure quality-of-life changes in clients. LOF scales are before-and-after tests (frequently unnormed) created by an agency or program to measure quality-of-life changes in clients. When it is used as an outcome performance measure, client satisfaction refers to client self-reporting about quality-of-life changes.

Different types of outcome performance measures are more or less amenable to measuring different types of client quality-of-life changes (see Table 6.3). For example, numeric counts are generally used to measure client conditions, status, or behaviors. Standardized measures are generally

TABLE 6.3 Types of Outcome Performance Measures and Different Approaches to Measuring Client Quality-of-Life Changes

• Numeric counts	Generally used to measure client conditions, status, and behaviors
• Standardized measures	Generally used to measure client feelings, attitudes, and perceptions
• Level of functioning scales	Generally used to measure client, or client family, functioning
• Client satisfaction	Generally used to measure client perceptions

TABLE 6.4 Intermediate and Ultimate Outcome Performance Measures

Intermediate Outcome Performance Measures	Ultimate Outcome Performance Measures
Numeric counts	Numeric counts
Standardized measures	Standardized measures
Level of functioning scales	Level of functioning scales
Client satisfaction	—

used to measure client perceptions, feelings, and attitudes. LOF scales are generally used to measure client, or client family, functioning. LOF scales are also used when standardized measures are not available or when they are not suitable for use with particular target populations because of age, ethnicity, or other factors. Finally, client satisfaction is generally used when measuring client perceptions about quality-of-life changes.

We reiterate that outcome performance measures are compiled and reported only on service completions (i.e., clients who complete treatment or who receive a full complement of services). For a review of the concept of a service completion and its importance for outcome performance measurement, please see Chapter 4.

INTERMEDIATE AND ULTIMATE OUTCOME PERFORMANCE MEASURES

The four types of outcome performance measures can also be divided into two broad categories depending on their use as either (a) intermediate outcome performance measures or (b) ultimate outcome performance measures. This is illustrated in Table 6.4.

Intermediate outcome performance measures assess quality-of-life changes in clients immediately on completion of treatment or receipt of a full complement of services. In other words, intermediate outcome performance measures provide an assessment of *treatment effects* (Else et al., 1992). Take, for example, the case of a child in residential care. An intermediate outcome performance measure attempts to assess quality-of-life changes (conditions or behaviors) in the child immediately on leaving the program or after receiving a full complement of services. But not all treatment effects are readily discernable immediately on completion of treatment or the receipt of a full complement of services (Benveniste, 1994). In addition, some stakeholders are interested in what might be called posttreatment effects or long-term effects (Else et al., 1992). Consequently, a need exists for some outcome performance measures to attempt to capture client quality-of-life data at some follow-up point (e.g., 3 months, 6 months, 1 year, etc.). In the case of a child in foster care, an ultimate outcome might be family reunification or adoption (Else et al., 1992). Some human service programs may use the same measure as both an intermediate outcome and an ultimate outcome; other human service programs may have different measures.

In theory, all four types of outcome performance measures can be used to capture data on either intermediate or ultimate outcomes. In actual practice, however, client satisfaction is rarely used as an ultimate outcome performance measure (Kettner & Martin, 1993; Kuechler et al., 1988; Nurius & Hudson, 1993). This finding may reflect a belief of human service administrators that client satisfaction data are more useful in assessing treatment effects and less useful in assessing posttreatment or long-term effects.

SELECTING OUTCOME
PERFORMANCE MEASURES

As was the case with the selection of output and quality performance measures, a three-step process is suggested for the development of outcome performance measures:

Step 1

A focus group broadly representative of the stakeholders of the human service program should be convened. Prior to meeting, the focus group's members should become familiar with the most recent and widely accepted research dealing with conceptual frameworks, theories, evaluations, and practice experience pertaining to the human service program.

Step 2

As many potential outcome performance measures as possible should be identified, discussed, and considered by the group. As part of this process, the social problem the human service program addresses and the assumptions made about the social problem should be made explicit.

Step 3

The group should arrive at a consensus on the one or two "best" outcome performance measures for the human service program.

CAUSE-AND-EFFECT RELATIONSHIPS

The use and reporting of outcome performance measures for human service programs imply a cause-and-effect relationship. A human service program is the cause, and the implied effect is a quality-of-life change in clients. This implied cause-and-effect relationship poses some potential problems for human service programs.

In discussing the implied cause-and-effect relationship between human service programs and outcome performance measures, the GASB (1994) offers a word of caution: "For many outcomes, a definite cause-and-effect relationship . . . cannot be established because of their complex nature and factors beyond the control of the entity [program] that affect the outcome being measured" (p. 22). GASB is saying that although an individual human service program may produce and report outcome performance measures, the program itself may not be the sole cause of the outcome. Consider the following scenario.

Twenty-five trainees in a job training program are hired into full-time employment immediately on graduating from the program. Twenty-five job placements (an outcome performance measure) are recorded and reported for the program. The same week the 25 trainees graduate, a major new manufacturing plant opens nearby and begins recruiting to fill 1,000 permanent full-time jobs. All 25 graduating trainees wind up hired by the new plant. Is the job training program the cause of the 25 trainees being employed? Or is the new manufacturing plant (a factor totally unrelated to the job training program) the cause of the 25 trainees being employed?

One could probably argue that both the job training program and the new plant are causes of the 25 trainees being employed. If the job training program had not adequately prepared the 25 trainees, they might not have been hired. Likewise, if the new manufacturing plant had not opened, the

25 trainees might not have been hired irrespective of how adequately the job training program had prepared them.

The point of this illustration is that the use of outcome performance measures by human service programs does not imply a one-to-one cause-and-effect relationship between the program and the outcome. The job training program should properly take credit for the job placements, but it should also work to ensure that its stakeholders understand that the program may not be the only cause. One might argue that human service programs should simply "take the credit" whenever possible and not bother with making disclaimers. The problem with this approach is illustrated by reversing the job training scenario. Suppose, for example, that the 25 trainees had graduated at the height of an economic recession, that the manufacturing plant never opened, and that only 5 (20%) of the graduating trainees found employment. Should the stakeholders of the job training program conclude that the program is ineffective? No, of course not! Factors other than the program, in this case a bad economy, affected the program's outcome performance measures—job placements. If human service programs do not want to shoulder 100% of the blame for the lack of program effectiveness due to factors beyond their control, it is probably wise not to take 100% of the credit.

Educating stakeholders about what outcome performance measures really are, and what they are not, is an important—and little discussed—problem associated with their use by human service programs. In a report describing initial findings from pilot outcome performance measurement projects conducted by federal departments under the Government Performance and Results Act (1993), the National Academy of Public Administration (Hatry & Wholey, 1994) comments that:

> outcome indicators will, in general, *not* tell the extent to which the program has actually caused the observed outcomes. . . . We suspect that the lack of understanding as to what the outcome indicators tell, and what they do not tell, will continue to cause confusion at all levels of the federal government and outside (e.g., with the media)—leading to excessive expectations as to what regular performance measurement can do. (p. 4)

SOCIAL INDICATORS AS ULTIMATE OUTCOME PERFORMANCE MEASURES

Some states and communities are experimenting with the idea of using social indicators as ultimate outcome performance measures for human service programs. Social indicators can be defined generally as data that enable evaluative judgments to be made about social problems in a community or state (Miller, 1991). Armed with social indicator data, citizens, advocacy groups, elected officials, and other stakeholders can make evaluative judgments about whether social problems in a community or state are getting better, getting worse, or staying about the same. Provided the same types of data are collected, comparisons can also be made between communities or states.

One of the more interesting experiments in the use of social indicators as outcome performance measures for human service programs is the state of Oregon's "Benchmarks" program. Oregon has developed—with a great deal of stakeholder input—a set of 272 benchmarks (Walters, 1994). Two features of the Oregon Benchmarks approach make it a particularly interesting case study.

First, many local municipal and county governments in Oregon, as well as the United Way of Portland, are following the lead of the state and have moved to adopt their own benchmarks (Walters, 1995). Some examples of the benchmarks developed by Multnomah County (Portland), Oregon, for its human service programs are shown in Table 6.5.

Second, in December 1994, after months of negotiation, the U.S. Department of Health and Human Services and the state of Oregon entered into an agreement called "Oregon Options." This demonstration project will use the Oregon Benchmarks to assess the results, impacts, and accomplishments of many of the federal human service programs that the state administers (Walters, 1995).

Although initiatives such as Oregon Benchmarks are certainly innovative and should be applauded, they also have a downside. The downside is, of course, the implied cause-and-effect relationships between human service programs and the social indicators that are used as ultimate outcome performance measures. An individual human service program is probably not going to have much effect on a social indicator. For example, one job training program—no matter how effective—is unlikely to have much effect on the unemployment rate.

One way to somewhat downplay the implied cause-and-effect relationships between individual human service programs and social indicators is to identify groups, or packages, of human service programs that all address the same social indicator. This grouping approach is proposed by the Florida Department of Health and Rehabilitative Services (FHRS). FHRS (1995) is experimenting with what it calls a "Service Tree" approach. The various human service programs that FHRS provides are to be related to a small number of specified indicators ($n = 38$), which in turn are to be related to an even smaller number ($n = 16$) of "core service tree outcomes."

TABLE 6.5 Example of Multnomah County, Oregon, "Benchmarks" for Human Service Programs

---

1. Adult mental health
   a. Percentage of clients who maintain or improve ability to function as measured by the Multnomah County Ability Scale
   b. Percentage of clients at high risk of hospitalization who are stable in community-based placements during a year's time
   c. Number of homeless clients with mental illness who are stabilized in housing
2. Children's mental health
   a. Percentage of runaway/displaced youth who successfully make a transition to stable housing
   b. Percentage of children receiving diversion services through family centers who do not have subsequent allegations of offenses
3. Alcohol and drugs
   a. Number of clients and their families who show a positive change in alcohol and/or drug-related behavior after receiving prevention services
   b. Number of clients who complete detoxification and who enroll in further alcohol or drug treatment
4. Antipoverty community action
   a. Number of case-managed households whose income available to meet basic needs has increased or stabilized
   b. Number of households receiving energy conservation assistance who report an increase in comfort or a decrease in energy consumption or energy expenditures

---

SOURCE: Adapted from Multnomah County, Oregon (1994).

Examples of some of the indicators and core service tree outcomes experimented with by FHRS are shown in Table 6.6.

Stressing the downside of using social indicators as ultimate outcome performance measures does not contradict the comments made in Chapter 3 about the importance of the link between performance measures and identified social problems. To say that performance measures should say something about, or relate to, identified social problems is one thing; to assess the effectiveness of human service programs on the basis of their impact on community or state social problems is something quite different.

OUTCOME PERFORMANCE MEASURES AND PROGRAMS OF SERVICES

In Chapter 4, the topic of programs of services was introduced. A program of services was defined as a human service program that is composed of multiple services or components. Adult day care was used as an example. Adult day care programs can include a transportation component, a meals

TABLE 6.6 The Florida Department of Health and Rehabilitative Services' "Service Tree" Approach

1. Outcome = Infant mortality
   Indicators:
      a. Infant mortality rates per 1000 live births
      b. Nonwhite infant mortality rates per 1000 live births
2. Outcome = Teenage pregnancy
   Indicators:
      a. Percentage of teenagers (15-19) giving birth
      b. Percentage of repeat teenagers (15-19) giving birth
3. Outcome = Early childhood education
   Indicators:
      a. Percentage of children entering kindergarten who require special education
4. Outcome = Drug-free Floridians
   Indicators:
      a. Adult and juvenile alcohol-related deaths per 100,000 population
      b. Adult and juvenile arrest rates for DUI and drug possession per 100,000 population
5. Outcome = Children growing up in permanent and stable families, free from abuse and neglect
   Indicators:
      a. Percentage of children reabused within 1 year of leaving children and family services
      b. Number of adoptive placements
6. Outcome = Economic self-sufficiency for families
   Indicators:
      a. Percentage of AFDC and food stamp recipients (under the age of 65) whose benefits are reduced or terminated because of increases in earnings and/or child support
      b. Average length of stay of AFDC

SOURCE: Adapted from Florida Department of Health and Rehabilitative Services (1995, pp. 5-7).

component, a socialization and recreation component, a health component, and others. We suggested that in developing and reporting intermediate output performance measures (units of service) for programs of services, it may be preferable to use separate intermediate outputs for each service or component. This approach, it was argued, has the benefit of providing more comprehensive and detailed pictures of programs of services.

When developing and reporting outcome performance measures (either intermediate or ultimate) for programs of services, however, the approach of using separate outcome measures for each service or component is not recommended. Outcome performance measures should be developed for programs of services as a whole and not for their constituent services or components. For most programs of services, an individual service or component by itself is not expected to achieve a quality-of-life change in clients.

Rather, it is the *combined effect* of the various services or components that is designed to bring about changes.

Continuing with the example of adult day care program, an outcome performance measure might be the number of at-risk older persons prevented from being prematurely institutionalized. Individually, none of the services or components of adult day care (transportation, meals, socialization and recreation, health, and others) can reasonably be expected to prevent premature institutionalization of at-risk older persons. But acting together as a program of services, adult day care can.

ASSESSING THE FOUR TYPES
OF OUTCOME PERFORMANCE MEASURES

An assessment of each of the four types of outcome performance measures will be made as each type is introduced: numeric counts (Chapter 7), standardized measures (Chapter 8), LOF scales (Chapter 9), and client satisfaction (Chapter 10). The assessment is based on seven criteria (utility, validity, reliability, precision, feasibility, cost, and unit cost reporting) suggested by previous research specifically relating to outcome performance measurement in human service programs (Kettner & Martin, 1993; Kettner et al., 1990; Kuechler et al., 1988; Millar & Millar, 1981; Nurius & Hudson, 1993; Rossi & Freeman, 1993; Tatara, 1980).

1. *Utility* refers to the extent to which the information generated by a particular type of outcome performance measure is considered useful and relevant to stakeholders (Millar & Millar, 1981; Nurius & Hudson, 1993). If stakeholders believe that the outcome performance measures adopted by a human service program do not provide useful effectiveness accountability information, then the resulting data will simply be ignored. Utility may well be the most important of the seven criteria in selecting outcome performance measures (Kuechler et al., 1988).

2. *Validity* refers to the extent to which a particular type of outcome performance measure really measures what it purports to measure (Rossi & Freeman, 1993). Validity is related to cause-and-effect relationships between human service programs and outcome performance measures. Sometimes, outcome performance measures may actually be measuring extraneous variables such as the influence of a new manufacturing plant opening in a community, or even the well-known Hawthorne effect, rather than the actual results, impacts, and accomplishments of human service programs. The less susceptible an outcome performance measure is to

being influenced by extraneous factors other than a human service program, the more valid the measure is.

3. *Reliability* refers to the extent to which a particular type of outcome performance measure produces the same results repeatedly (Rossi & Freeman, 1993). As a general rule, the more standardized the outcome performance measure, the more reliable it is.

4. *Precision* refers to the extent to which a type of outcome performance measure captures incremental (either quantitative or qualitative) changes in the quality of life of clients. Precision is directly related to the level of measurement used by an outcome performance measure. Interval level data are more precise than ordinal data. Ordinal data are more precise than nominal data.

5. *Feasibility* refers to the extent to which political, ethical, administrative, personnel, or other factors may hinder or prevent the use of a particular type of outcome performance measure (Millar & Millar, 1981). The issue here is whether a proposed outcome performance measure is practical. For example, and as a general rule, the more administrative processing time required by a particular type of outcome performance measure, the less feasible it becomes because of demands on staff time.

6. *Cost* refers to the start-up and maintenance costs of a particular type of outcome performance measure in relation to the other types (Millar & Millar, 1981).

7. *Unit cost reporting* refers to the ability to generate cost per outcome data (Kettner & Martin, 1993; Kettner et al., 1990). Outcome performance measures developed with the expectation of satisfying service efforts and accomplishments reporting (GASB, 1994) must be capable of reporting costs per unit of outcome. Some types of outcome performance measures, such as numeric counts, lend themselves more readily to this type of cost analysis than do others.

Each type of outcome performance measure (numeric count, standardized measures, LOF scales, and client satisfaction) is rated on each of these seven criteria using a *high, medium, low* scale. The selection of what type or types of outcome performance measures may be best suited to an individual human service program involves not only an individual assessment of all seven criteria but also an assessment of trade-offs between criteria. For example, a human service program might decide on a little less validity and reliability for significantly less cost.

This chapter has provided a general introduction to the topic of outcome performance measures. Chapter 7 will now examine in detail the first of the four major types of outcome performance measures: numeric counts.

Chapter 7

NUMERIC COUNTS

INTRODUCTION

Numeric counts are the first of the four major types of outcome performance measures to be discussed in detail. Numeric counts resemble output performance measures and outputs with quality dimensions but with important differences. Because of the similarity in appearance, numeric counts represent a natural bridge to a detailed discussion of outcome performance measures.

WHAT ARE NUMERIC COUNTS?

Unfortunately, no universally accepted definition of numeric counts exists. Some of the definitions proposed include the following:

1. Numeric counts "include measures such as demographic and characteristic data and information related to client flow. Examples of these nominal measures include number of children who return home following residential treatment; number of chemical dependency halfway house clients who are chemically free at one-year follow-up" (Kuechler et al., 1988, p. 74).

2. Numeric counts "are nominal measures relating to client flow. They require yes or no answers to specific questions, such as the following: Was the client placed in a job following WIN training? Did the child return home following residential treatment?" (Kettner et al., 1990, p. 119).

3. Numeric counts are critical events that "reflect an undesirable occurrence that an agency is trying to prevent or a desirable occurrence that an

TABLE 7.1 Examples of Numeric Counts Used as Outcome Performance Measures

1. Information and Referral
   a   Intermediate outcome performance measure   One client receiving assistance
   b. Ultimate outcome performance measure   None
2. Home-Delivered Meals
   a. Intermediate outcome performance measure   One client maintaining good
                                                        nutrition
   b. Ultimate outcome performance measure   One client maintained in own home
3. Counseling
   a. Intermediate outcome performance measure   One client demonstrating improve-
                                                        ment in condition or behavior
   b. Ultimate outcome performance measure   One client no longer in need of
                                                        counseling

agency is attempting to achieve. Desirable events include: a client becoming employed and no longer in need of services, a child returned home or adopted. Undesirable events include: a recurrence of confirmed child abuse, a re-referral after a client's case has been closed as successful, arrests of juvenile clients" (Millar & Millar, 1981, p. 27).

On the basis of these proposed definitions, numeric counts can be said to possess two characteristics that set them apart from other types of outcome performance measures. First, they represent simple "head counts" of how many clients achieve a quality-of-life change as a result of a human service program. Second, they are dichotomous (yes/no) measures in which a quality-of-life change either occurs or does not occur for a given client. Varying degrees of outcome, either quantitative or qualitative, are not recognized.

EXAMPLES OF NUMERIC COUNTS

Table 7.1 illustrates the use of numeric counts as outcome performance measures for the continuing program examples of information and referral, home-delivered meals, and counseling. The examples include the use of numeric counts as both intermediate and ultimate outcomes.

Some aspects of Table 7.1 warrant additional explanation. First, no ultimate outcome performance measure is shown for information and referral. A few human service programs—and particularly those that deal with linkage activities such as information and referral and specialized transportation services—do not lend themselves well to the development of ultimate outcome performance measures. The ultimate purposes for which clients use information and referral and specialized transportation are simply too varied.

Second, the implied cause-and-effect relationship between the home-delivered meals program and the intermediate and ultimate outcome performance measures shown is tenuous at best. The point about the implied cause-and-effect relationship between a human service program and its outcome performance measures was stressed in Chapter 6 but is worth repeating. In this case, a home-delivered meals program may assist an individual in maintaining good nutrition or in maintaining an independent living status but is hardly sufficient to achieve these desired end states by itself. A package of services including—at a minimum—homemaker and visiting nurse as well as home-delivered meals would more likely be required. Although home-delivered meals programs do not by themselves enable clients to be maintained in their own homes, they do contribute to this desirable end state, and thus the measure is appropriate for use as an ultimate outcome. The same point can be made for the intermediate outcome performance measure shown for the information and referral program. Factors beyond the control of information and referral programs affect whether clients ultimately receive services from referral agencies. Nevertheless, information and referral programs exist to link clients in need with agencies that can meet those needs. Consequently, the number of clients who ultimately receive assistance from referral agencies is an appropriate outcome performance measure for an information and referral program even if the implied cause-and-effect relationship is tenuous.

Third, a potentially confusing resemblance may exist between the numeric counts shown in Table 7.1 and final output performance measures (units of service) and quality performance measures (outputs with quality dimensions) shown in earlier chapters. To highlight the differences, Table 7.2 brings together all three types of performance measures (outputs, quality, and numeric counts outcomes) for the three human service programs.

Table 7.2 shows that output, quality, and outcome performance measures really measure different dimensions of a human service program. The numeric count *outcome* performance measures for all three human service programs have a *client focus,* whereas the *output* and *quality* performance measures have a *service focus.* The output performance measures are designed to capture information about how much service is provided by each program. The quality performance measures are designed to capture information about the quality of the service provided by each program. The numeric counts outcome performance measures are designed to provide information on the results, impacts, or accomplishments of each program as measured by client quality-of-life changes.

TABLE 7.2 Contrasting Output, Quality, and Outcome Performance Measures

1. Information and Referral
   a. Intermediate output performance measure (unit of service) — One referral
   b. Output with quality dimension — One appropriate referral
   c. Outcome performance measure
      (1) Intermediate — One client receiving assistance
2. Home-Delivered Meals
   a. Intermediate output performance measure (unit of service) — One meal
   b. Output with quality dimension — One meal delivered hot
   c. Outcome performance measure
      (1) Intermediate — One client maintaining good nutrition
      (2) Ultimate — One client maintained in own home
3. Counseling
   a. Intermediate output performance measure (unit of service) — One hour
   b. Output measure with quality dimension — One hour with counselor of record
   c. Outcome performance measure
      (1) Intermediate — One client demonstrating improvement in condition or behavior
      (2) Ultimate — One client no longer in need of counseling

THE FLORIDA DEPARTMENT OF HEALTH AND REHABILITATIVE SERVICES

In 1989, we spent the summer working with top and middle managers of the FHRS to facilitate the development of numeric counts as outcome performance measures for a number of human service programs. FHRS staff developed initial numeric counts for each of five major groupings of human service programs: (a) aging and adult services; (b) alcohol, drug, and mental health services; (c) employment services; (d) services to children, youth, and families; and (e) services for persons who are developmentally disabled.

Some representative examples of the numeric counts developed by FHRS are illustrated below. The numeric counts shown are not necessarily the only ones that could be used for the identified human service programs, nor are they necessarily the best possible choices. The examples are presented simply to demonstrate how one human service organization began the task of thinking about numeric counts as outcome performance measures.

Aging and Adult Services

1. Adult day care services
   a. One client returned to independent living status
   b. One client prevented from entering a long-term care facility
   c. One client entering a nursing home facility
2. Case management
   a. One client maintained in own home
   b. One client returned to independent living status
   c. One client no longer needing services
3. Congregate meals
   a. One client maintained in own home
   b. One client returned to independent living status
   c. One client no longer needing services
4. Displaced homemaker program
   a. One client employed (full-time or part-time)
5. Home-delivered meals program
   a. One client maintained in own home
   b. One client returned to independent living status
   c. One client no longer needing services
6. Homemaker services
   a. One client maintained in own home
   b. One client returned to independent living status
   c. One client no longer needing services

Alcohol, Drug, and Mental Health

1. Adult residential treatment
   a. One client abstaining from drugs and/or alcohol
   b. One client regularly taking medication
   c. One client having contact with the criminal justice system
   d. One client requiring hospitalization for medical treatment
   e. One client recidivating

Employment Services

1. Training
   a. One client finding employment
   b. One client remaining employed for a minimum of 6 months, 1 year, etc.

Developmental Disabilities

1. Behavior management
   a. One client reported to be exhibiting maladaptive behavior(s)
   b. One client with a current behavior checklist in his or her case file

Children, Youth, and Families

1. Day care
   a. One client able to find or maintain employment because of day care
   b. One client no longer needing service
2. Child abuse and neglect
   a. One client no longer abusing or neglecting his or her children
3. Delinquency nonresidential
   a. One client having contact with the juvenile justice system
   b. One client having a referral for a new law violation within 12 months
   c. One client having a felony referral
   d. One client currently enrolled in school
   e. One client currently attending classes
   f. One client maintaining passing grades in school
4. Emergency shelter
   a. One client returned to own home
   b. One client arrested for status offenses within 12 months after leaving shelter
   c. One client transferred to other out-of-home care
5. Intensive crisis counseling
   a. One client with no reported incidence of family violence

THE PREFERENCE FOR NUMERIC COUNTS

Examples of outcome performance measures used in the SEA reporting documents released to date by the GASB (1993, 1994) are virtually all numeric counts. Likewise, in reports evaluating pilot projects on SEA reporting at the state and local government levels, the overwhelming number of examples presented are again numeric counts (e.g., Carpenter, Ruchala, & Waller, 1991; Hatry, Fountain, Sullivan, & Kremer, 1990). Because of these influences, state and local government human service agencies moving to implement SEA reporting also are demonstrating a strong preference for numeric counts. For example, attempts at implementing SEA reporting for human service programs in the City of Phoenix,

TABLE 7.3 Assessment of Numeric Counts as an Outcome Performance Measure

• Utility	High
• Validity	Low to medium
• Reliability	High
• Precision	Low
• Feasibility	High
• Cost	Low to medium
• Unit cost reporting	High

Arizona (1992), in Palm Beach County, Florida (1994), and in Multnomah County, Oregon (1993), all show a clear preference for the use of numeric counts as outcome performance measures.

Reports dealing with initial pilot projects on the development of outcome performance measures for federal programs under the Government Performance and Results Act (1993) also demonstrate preferences for numeric counts (e.g., Hatry & Wholey, 1994). Finally, some of the research on client outcome monitoring in human service programs similarly suggests a preference for numeric counts as outcome performance measures. Millar and Millar (1981), for example, suggest that numeric counts should be used as outcome performance measures by all human service programs. Kuechler et al. (1988) suggest that numeric counts may be preferred by human service programs because they are relatively easy to define, use, and interpret.

Numeric counts appear to be the outcome performance measures of choice for government programs, including government human service programs. This preference poses a problem. What happens if a particular human service program prefers to use standardized measures, LOF scales, or client satisfaction as an outcome performance measure but must report to a government funding source or some other stakeholder using numeric counts? The answer is to find a method of translating standardized measures, LOF scales, and client satisfaction into numeric counts. Chapters 8, 9, and 10 dealing with standardized measures, LOF scales, and client satisfaction each contains a section suggesting methods by which these other types of outcome performance measures can be translated into numeric counts.

AN ASSESSMENT
OF NUMERIC COUNTS

Table 7.3 rates numeric counts as outcome performance measures. The assessment includes the criteria of the utility, validity, reliability, precision, feasibility, costs, and unit cost reporting ability of numeric counts.

The *utility* of using numeric counts as an outcome performance measure is rated as *high*. Because so many important classes of stakeholders appear to prefer numeric counts over the other types of outcome performance measures, their ultimate acceptance and use should be considerable. The *validity* of using numeric counts is rated as *low* to *medium*. The validity of numeric counts depends largely on the extent to which the implied cause-and-effect relationship between an individual human service program and its numeric counts is in fact a real and direct relationship. Do the numeric counts selected for use as outcome performance measures really measure client quality-of-life changes due to participation in human service programs? Or do they measure other factors as well? The same dichotomous yes/no nature that gives numeric counts its high rating on utility poses significant validity problems. It is difficult, and often inaccurate, to reduce client quality-of-life changes to black/white, yes/no categories. An additional validity problem is that numeric counts data are frequently generated from agency files and reports that are notoriously incomplete and error-prone (Millar & Millar, 1981).

The *reliability* of using numeric counts is rated as *high*. The simple dichotomous nature of numeric counts ("yes" the client did achieve a quality-of-life change as defined by the numeric count, or "no" the client did not) should result in a high degree of interrater reliability as well as a high degree of reliability through time.

The *precision* of numeric counts is rated as *low*. Because of its nominal yes/no nature, numeric counts do not deal with varying degrees (either quantitatively or qualitatively) of quality-of-life changes in clients. Thus, numeric counts are significantly less precise than some of the other types of outcome performance measures.

The *feasibility* of using numeric counts is rated as *high*. Numeric counts are easy to develop and interpret. The nature of numeric counts is also such that ethical problems involving client confidentiality are avoided. Administratively, the use of numeric counts—particularly when data that can serve as numeric counts are already being collected—should not pose any significant problems. Finally, political factors should probably work to the advantage of numeric counts, given the strength of the apparent stakeholder support for this type of outcome performance measure.

The *cost* of using numeric counts is rated *low* to *medium*. The cost is low if data that can be used as numeric counts are already being collected, medium if additional data must be collected and if forms must be redesigned and computer programs altered.

The *unit cost reporting* ability of numeric counts is rated as *high*. Unit cost reporting is in fact tailor-made for numeric counts because they can be expressed as simple nominal counts.

On balance, numeric counts tend to hold up well against the assessment criteria. They are easy to use, report, and interpret, but they are less precise and valid than other types of outcome performance measures. In sum, numeric counts score well on the criterion of utility but at the expense of the criteria of precision and validity. If a human service program would rather increase the precision and validity of the outcome performance measures it uses and is willing to sacrifice some utility, standardized measures and/or LOF scales may be the more appropriate choice. In Chapter 8, the discussion focuses on standardized measures, the most valid and precise of the four types of outcome performance measures.

Chapter 8

STANDARDIZED MEASURES

INTRODUCTION

As discussed in Chapter 7, numeric counts have many advantages as outcome performance measures. They also have some disadvantages, however. The major disadvantage is the inability of numeric counts to capture varying degrees of client quality-of-life changes.

Some human service programs may need more sensitive outcome performance measures than are provided by the yes/no, black/white nature of numeric counts. For example, human service programs that involve clinical assessments and interventions may need more sensitive outcome performance measures that are capable of tracking degrees of client improvement. Standardized measures are probably the most sensitive of the four types of outcome performance measures.

WHAT ARE STANDARDIZED MEASURES?

Standardized measures are validated, reliable, and normed before-and-after tests used to assess quality-of-life changes in clients. Some standardized measures focus on both the client and the client's family. Standardized measures are frequently available for general use but often at a price. Many standardized measures are copyrighted and can be used only with permission of the copyright holder, who frequently charges a fee.

Standardized measures share two common features. First, they generally consist of a set of structured questions designed to solicit information about clients—and sometimes about client families—on conditions, behaviors, attitudes, feelings, intra- or interpersonal functioning, personality development, and other dimensions. Second, they generally include a set of uniform procedures for administration and scoring, usually yielding a single numerical score that is useful in estimating the magnitude, intensity, or degree of the dimension measured (Leavitt & Reid, 1981).

Some standardized measures, such as many of those developed by Hudson (1992), include a *clinical cutting score*. If a client's score on a standard measure is above this threshold, a clinical condition is said to exist. For example, Hudson's (1992) Index of Marital Satisfaction has a clinical cutting score of 30. If a client's score on this standardized measure is above 30, then the client has a clinical condition.

A few standardized measures are lengthy and attempt in-depth assessments of clients. Others, called rapid assessment instruments (RAIs), tend to be brief. This brevity may account for the popularity of RAIs. Many of the standardized measures used as outcome performance measures in human service programs are RAIs. Leavitt and Reid (1981) identify 11 characteristics that distinguish RAIs from other standardized measures:

1. They are self-report measures, filled out by the client.
2. They tend to be short (one or two pages), easy to administer, and easy to complete (usually in less than 15 minutes).
3. They are generally written in a clear, simple language that the client can understand.
4. They can be scored rapidly, often in the presence of the client.
5. The interpretation of the measure is straightforward and clear.
6. The use of the measure by the practitioner does not require extensive knowledge of testing procedures.
7. They do not require subscription to a particular theoretical perspective.
8. They provide a systematic overview of the client's problem as well as information on individual aspects that may be discussed in the interview.
9. The overall score provides an index of the degree, intensity, or magnitude of the client's problem.
10. They can provide a structured means for collecting data that is standardized and comparable across applications of the measure, both for individual clients and across all clients.
11. They can be used on a one-time basis or as repeated measures, thereby producing information on changes in the client's problem over time by comparing scores from one administration to another. The scores obtained can be plotted on a single-system design chart, allowing easy, visual inspection of changes. (Quoted in Fischer & Corcoran, 1994, pp. 35-36)

TABLE 8.1 A Sample Rapid Assessment Instrument

INDEX OF CLINICAL STRESS (ICS)

Name: _____ Today's Date: _____

This questionnaire is designed to measure the way you feel about the amount of personal stress that you experience. It is not a test, so there are no right or wrong answers. Answer each item as carefully and as accurately as you can by placing a number beside each one as follows.

1 = None of the time
2 = Very rarely
3 = A little of the time
4 = Some of the time
5 = A good part of the time
6 = Most of the time
7 = All of the time

1. ____ I feel extremely tense.
2. ____ I feel very jittery.
3. ____ I feel like I want to scream.
4. ____ I feel overwhelmed.
5. ____ I feel very relaxed.
6. ____ I feel so anxious I want to cry.
7. ____ I feel so stressed that I'd like to hit something.
8. ____ I feel very calm and peaceful.
9. ____ I feel like I am stretched to the breaking point.
10. ____ It is very hard for me to relax.
11. ____ It is very easy for me to fall asleep at night.
12. ____ I feel an enormous sense of pressure on me.
13. ____ I feel like my life is going very smoothly.
14. ____ I feel very panicked.
15. ____ I feel like I am on the verge of a total collapse.
16. ____ I feel that I am losing control of my life.
17. ____ I feel that I am near a breaking point.
18. ____ I feel wound up like a coiled spring.
19. ____ I feel that I can't keep up with all the demands on me.
20. ____ I feel very much behind in my work.
21. ____ I feel tense and angry with those around me.
22. ____ I feel I must race from one task to the next.
23. ____ I feel that I just can't keep up with everything.
24. ____ I feel as tight as a drum.
25. ____ I feel very much on edge.

Copyright (c) 1990, Walter W. Hudson & Neil Abell   Illegal to Photocopy or Otherwise Reproduce

5, 8, 11, 13

SOURCE: Hudson (1992, p. 34). Copyright © 1990 by Walter W. Hudson and Neil Abell. Illegal to photocopy or otherwise reproduce. Reprinted by permission.

Table 8.1 is an example of a rapid assessment instrument used to assess clinical stress in clients.

TYPES OF STANDARDIZED MEASURES

Standardized measures vary in a number of ways discussed below. These include (a) substantive focus, (b) who completes them, and (c) the construction of their response scales.

SUBSTANTIVE FOCUS

As Table 8.2 demonstrates, standardized measures vary widely in their focus. For example, a standardized measure can focus on a *population,* such as children, couples, families, adults, or older persons. The Family Assessment Device (FAD) is an example of a standardized measure that focuses on a population. Other standardized measures focus on *behavior.* Violence, parenting behaviors, job-seeking behaviors, health-related practices, assertiveness, and many other behaviors can be assessed using standardized measures. Another variation is by *attitude.* Attitudes toward self, children, and significant others, for example, are used in counseling clients and client families.

Standardized measures can also have a *problem* focus. Problems such as use of drugs and alcohol, physical health, social dysfunction, and ability to perform basic activities of daily living can all be assessed with standardized measures. In addition, Hudson (1990) has developed a Multi-Problem Screening Inventory (MPSI). Some standardized measures focus on *intrapersonal* or *interpersonal functioning.* Intrapersonal functioning measures include such areas as temperament, self-esteem, thoughts, and depression, whereas interpersonal functioning measures deal with the ability of clients to relate to others including family members and other social contacts.

A number of standardized measures used with children have *development* as their focus. Others, such as the well-known Minnesota Multiphasic Personality Inventory (MMPI), focus on *personality traits* in an effort to produce a personality profile. A number of standardized measures used in job training programs focus on such factors as *achievement, knowledge,* and *aptitude.* Finally, some standardized measures have a *services* focus (e.g., child day care and foster care). This listing is meant to be illustrative, not exhaustive, and the categories are not necessarily mutually exclusive.

WHO COMPLETES THEM?

Standardized measures also differ according to who completes them. Many standardized measures are designed to be completed by clients. For example, Hudson's (1992) personal adjustment measures are completed by

TABLE 8.2 Focus of Standardized Measures

Focus	Example
Population	Young Children's Social Desirability Scale (YCSD) 26-item scale for measuring young children's need for social approval
Problem	Child Abuse Potential (CAP) Inventory 160-item scale for measuring potential for child abuse in parents and prospective parents
Behavior	Preschool Behavior Rating Scale Set of 20 scales rating preschool development on several dimensions
Attitude	Maryland Parent Attitude Survey (MPAS) 95-item scale for measuring attitudes of parents toward child rearing
Intrapersonal functioning	Generalized Expectancy for Success Scale Measures an individual's belief in ability to attain goals
Interpersonal functioning	Index of Family Relations 25-item scale for measuring family relationships
Development	Developmental Profile II 186-item scale for measuring child development up to age 9
Personality traits	Liking People Scale Measures whether an individual approaches or avoids social interaction
Achievement	Career Skills Assessment Program Measures student competency in areas important to career development
Knowledge	Knowledge Scale 73-item scale for measuring a parent's knowledge of appropriate growth and behavior in children up to age 2
Aptitude	Differential Aptitude Tests An integrated series of measures for assessing verbal reasoning, spelling, need for education, and vocation guidance
Services	Seattle/King County Four C's Evaluation Checklist for In-Home Care, Day Care Homes, and Day Care Centers Measures child health and nutrition and staff-child interactions

NOTE: A bibliographic reference for each of these scales appears at the end of this chapter.

clients themselves. These measures help to determine how clients perceive their own behaviors and feelings in a range of areas. Still other standardized measures are designed to be completed by professionals or knowledgeable third parties. A number of standardized measures used to assess the ability of older clients to perform activities of daily living can be completed by the client, a caregiver, a relative, or a professional (Fillenbaum, 1985; Katz, Ford, & Moskowitz, 1963; Mahoney & Barthel, 1965).

RESPONSE SCALES

Standardized measures also vary in the construction of their response scales. The majority of standardized measures use Likert-type scales with response categories indicating frequency. Most of Hudson's (1992) standardized measures use a 7-point scale in which 1 = *none of the time*, 2 = *very rarely*, 3 = *a little of the time*, 4 = *some of the time*, 5 = *a good part of the time*, 6 = *most of the time*, and 7 = *all of the time*. The Marital Communications Skills Rating Scale (Franklin, 1982) offers a scale from 1 to 10 with the single descriptors of *inadequate* at the low end and *adequate* at the high end. Other response scales provide brief descriptions at the extremes and ask respondents to select the level that most accurately describes the client.

USING STANDARDIZED MEASURES AS OUTCOME PERFORMANCE MEASURES

The use of standardized measures as outcome performance measures for human service programs requires several actions. First, the type and number of standardized measures to be used in a human service program must be determined. As is the case with all performance measures, stakeholders should be involved in the selection process.

Second, all clients must be assessed using the selected standardized measures at the point of entry into the human service program. This action may appear to depart from previous statements made in this book that outcome performance measures data are collected and reported only for clients who complete treatment or receive a full complement of services. The inclusion of this action is not a contradiction. The use of the selected standardized measures with all clients entering a human service program is necessary to establish an individual client baseline profile. Because it is impossible to know which clients will complete treatment and which ones will drop out, a baseline profile must be developed for all clients.

Third, clients participate in the human service program. Fourth, the selected standardized measures are again administered to those clients who complete treatment or receive a full complement of services. If the standardized measures are used to create a treatment profile of a client *immediately* on completion of treatment or receipt of a full complement of services, the resulting data become intermediate outcome performance measures. When the standardized measures are used to create a posttreatment profile of a client (i.e., at some follow-up point), the resulting data become ultimate outcome performance measures.

Fifth, a comparison is made between each individual client's baseline profile and the client's treatment profile or posttreatment profile. If a client demonstrates either *measurable* movement toward desirable conditions, status, behaviors, functioning, attitudes, feelings, or perceptions or *measurable* movement away from undesirable conditions, status, behaviors, functioning, attitudes, feelings, or perceptions, then the client has experienced a quality-of-life change.

TRANSLATING STANDARDIZED MEASURES INTO NUMERIC COUNTS

Because performance measurement uses programs as its unit of analysis, a process must be developed to aggregate individual client standardized measures to the level of human service programs. In considering how to translate standardized measures into numeric counts, it is useful to divide all clients who have completed treatment or received a full complement of services into two groups: (a) clients demonstrating improvement and (b) others. Persons working with data on the clients who demonstrate improvement can develop numeric counts using the following categories:

1. the number of clients who demonstrate measurable improvement;
2. the proportion (e.g., % = 67) of clients who demonstrate measurable improvement to the total number (e.g., $n = 100$) of clients completing treatment or receiving a full complement of services;
3. the number of clients who demonstrate clinical improvement. Clinical improvement can be defined as a client who was above a clinical cutting score on the client baseline profile but was below the clinical cutting score on either the treatment profile or the posttreatment profile;
4. the proportion of clients who demonstrate clinical improvement to the total number of clients who complete treatment or receive a full complement of services;
5. the number of clients who achieve a target level of improvement;
6. the proportion of clients who achieve a target level of improvement to the total number of clients who completed treatment or received a full complement of services and who had an established target level of improvement.

The concept of a target level of improvement requires some additional explanation. Some clients may voluntarily establish a desired target level of improvement for themselves. For example, a married couple may wish to improve their marital satisfaction. Using Hudson's (1992) Index of Marital Satisfaction, the couple may score 50 on the baseline profile and contract with their therapist to reduce the score to 40. If the treatment or posttreatment profile score is 40 or less, the couple have achieved their

TABLE 8.3 Assessment of Standardized Measures as an Outcome Performance Measure

• Utility	Low to high
• Validity	High
• Reliability	High
• Precision	Medium to high
• Feasibility	Low
• Cost	High
• Unit cost reporting	Low

target level of improvement. This same approach can also be used with involuntary clients (clients placed into a human service program by the court, a school district, a government agency, a parent, etc.).

In human service programs that use multiple standardized measures, numeric count data can be aggregated and reported for each dimension captured by each standardized measure. For example, in an in-home service program for older persons that uses multiple standardized measures, it might be more appropriate to aggregate and report numeric count data that identify client improvement by each standardized measure used (e.g., activities of daily living, social contacts, physical health, etc.). This approach also has the benefit of communicating more outcome performance measurement data to stakeholders.

AN ASSESSMENT
OF STANDARDIZED MEASURES

Table 8.3 shows an assessment of the use of standardized measures as outcome performance measures. As was the case with numeric counts, the criteria of utility, validity, reliability, precision, feasibility, cost, and unit cost reporting are used.

The *utility* of using standardized measures as an outcome performance measure is rated as *low* to *high*. Data generated by standardized measures have *high* utility for stakeholders such as direct service staff and program administrators but *low* utility for other stakeholders (e.g., citizens, elected officials, and funding sources) who are generally unfamiliar with their use, scoring, and interpretation.

Both the *validity* and *reliability* of standardized measures are rated as *high*. Standardized measures are by definition valid and reliable measures. Remember, however, that reliability and validity levels established across many clients may not necessarily hold for any one particular client. In addition, a single standardized measure may be insufficiently sensitive to capture all important client dimensions.

The *precision* of standardized measures is rated as *medium* to *high*, depending on the individual standardized measure used and the number of items that compose its scale. Some standardized measures are more precise than others. A standardized measure that uses 25 items to assess clinical anxiety, such as Hudson's (1992) scale, will probably be more precise than another standardized measure that uses only 5 or 10 items.

The *feasibility* of using standardized measures is rated as *low*. Many standardized measures must be purchased. Staff must also be oriented and trained in their administration and interpretation. Staff time must also be devoted to their use and scoring as well as to the aggregation of data to the program level.

The *cost* of using standardized measures is rated as *high* for all the reasons stated above. The *unit cost reporting* ability of standardized measures is rated as *low*. In pure form, it is questionable how much relevant unit cost reporting information is supplied by standardized measures. For example, the knowledge that it costs an average of $1,200 to decrease a client's score by one point—or even several points—on a standardized measure is hard to interpret.

RESOURCES FOR USE IN
SELECTING STANDARDIZED MEASURES

The remainder of this chapter is devoted to identifying sources of standardized measures. First, three major reference books are described that cover a wide range of standardized measures available for use in clinical assessments. Next, a listing of standardized measures for use with specific services and target populations is presented covering (a) services to families and children, (b) employment-related services, and (c) services to older persons.

SOURCES OF SELECTED CLINICAL
STANDARDIZED MEASURES

Reference: Fischer, J., & Corcoran, K. (1994). *Measures for clinical practice: Vol. 1. Couples, families and children.* New York: Free Press.
Reference: Fischer, J., & Corcoran, K. (1994). *Measures for clinical practice: Vol. 2. Adults.* New York: Free Press.
Reference: Jordan, C., & Franklin, C. (1995). *Clinical assessment for social workers.* Chicago: Lyceum.

SOURCES OF SELECTED STANDARDIZED
MEASURES FOR SERVICES TO FAMILIES AND CHILDREN

General References

Reference: Magura, S., & Moses, B. S. (1987). *Outcome measures for child welfare services.*
Washington, DC: Child Welfare League of America.

Reference: Magura, S., Moses, B. S., & Jones, M. A. (1987). *Assessing risk and measuring change in families: The family risk scales.* Washington, DC: Child Welfare League of America.

Standardized Measures for Use With Young Children

Measure: Developmental Profile II

Source: Psychological Development Publications, P. O. Box 3198, Aspen, CO 81611.

Measure: Environmental Standards Profile: Method of Assessing Quality Group Care and Education of Young Children

Source: W. Fowler, Department of Applied Psychology, Ontario Institute for Studies in Education, 252 Bloor St. West, Toronto, Ontario, Canada.

Measure: Preschool Behavior Rating Scale

Source: Barker, W. F., & Doeff, A. M. (1980). *Preschool behavior rating scale: Administration and scoring manual.* New York: Child Welfare League of America.

Measure: Seattle/King County Four C's Evaluation Checklists for In-Home Care, Day Care Homes, and Day Care Centers

Source: King County Child Care Coordinating Committee. (n.d.). *In-home care checklist, day care home checklist, day care center checklist.* Washington, DC: Day Care and Child Development Council of America.

Measure: Young Children's Social Desirability Scale (YCSD)

Source: Ford, L. H., & Rubin, B. M. (1970). A social desirability questionnaire for young children. *Journal of Consulting and Clinical Psychology, 35,* 195-204.

Standardized Measures for Use With Parents and Children

Measure: Adult-Adolescent Parenting Inventory (AAPI)

Source: S. J. Bavolek, Family Development Associates, P.O. Box 94365, Schaumberg, IL 60194.

Measure: Maryland Parent Attitude Survey (MPAS)

Source: D. K. Pumroy, College of Education, University of Maryland, College Park, MD 20742.

Measure: Parent-Child Interaction Rating Procedure (P-CIRP)

Source: Institute for Family and Child Study, Home Management Unit No. 2, Michigan State University, East Lansing, MI 48824.

Measure: Parental Contact Scale

Source: J. W. Hollander, Department of Psychology, Emory University, Atlanta, GA 30322.

Standardized Measures for Use With Families

Measure: Family Assessment Device (FAD)

Source: Family Research Program, Butler Hospital, 345 Blackstone Blvd., Providence, RI 92906.

Measure: Family Functioning Scale
Source: L. L. Geismar, Graduate School of Social Work, Rutgers University, New Brunswick, NJ 08903.
Measure: Family Service Association Follow-Up Questionnaire
Source: Family Service Association of America, 11700 West Lake Park Drive, Park Place, Milwaukee, WI 53224.
Measure: Index of Family Relations
Source: Hudson, W. H. (1982). *The clinical measurement package: A field manual.* Chicago: Dorsey Press.
Measure: Self-Report Family Instrument (SFI)
Source: W. R. Beavers, M.D., Southwest Family Institute, 12532 Nuestra, Dallas, TX 75230.

Standardized Measures for Education and Training

Measure: Child Abuse Potential (CAP) Inventory
Source: J. S. Milner, Department of Psychology, Western Carolina University, Cullowhee, NC 28723.
Measure: Knowledge Scale
Source: A. S. Epstein, High/Scope Educational Research Foundation, 600 North River St., Ypsilanti, MI 48197.
Measure: Parenting Stress Index
Source: R. R. Abidin, Institute of Clinical Psychology, University of Virginia, Charlottesville, VA 22903.

SOURCES OF SELECTED STANDARDIZED MEASURES FOR EMPLOYMENT-RELATED SERVICES

Standardized Measures for Use With Work Attitudes and Skills

Measure: Career Skills Assessment Program
Source: Krumboltz, J. D., & Hamel, D. A. (Eds.). (1982). *Assessing career development.* Palo Alto, CA: Mayfield.
Measure: National Assessment of Education Progress
Source: Krumboltz, J. D., & Hamel, D. A. (Eds.). (1982). *Assessing career development.* Palo Alto, CA: Mayfield.
Measure: Job Training Assessment Program
Source: Kapes, J. T., & Mastie, M. M. (Eds.). (1982). *A counselor's guide to vocational guidance instruments.* Falls Church, VA: National Vocational Guidance Association.

Standardized Measures for Use in Literacy Testing

Measure: Differential Aptitude Tests
Source: Mastie, M. M. (1979). Review of the differential aptitude tests. *Measurement and Evaluation in Guidance, 2,* 87-95.
Measure: General Aptitude Test Battery
Source: Angrisani, A. (1982). *U.S. Employment Service tests and assessment techniques* (USES Test Research Report No. 32). Washington, DC: U.S. Employment Service.
Measure: Test of Adult Basic Education
Source: Kapes, J. T., & Mastie, M. M. (Eds.). (1982). *A counselor's guide to vocational guidance instruments.* Falls Church, VA: National Vocational Guidance Association.

Measure: Adult Basic Learning Education
Source: Kapes, J. T., & Mastie, M. M. (Eds.). (1982). *A counselor's guide to vocational guidance instruments*. Falls Church, VA: National Vocational Guidance Association.

Standardized Measures for Use in Testing Social/Communication Skills

Measure: Career Skills Assessment Program
Source: Krumboltz, J. D., & Hamel, D. A. (Eds.). (1982). *Assessing career development*. Palo Alto, CA: Mayfield.
Measure: Liking People Scale
Source: Filsinger, E. E. (1981). A measure of interpersonal orientation: The Liking People Scale. *Journal of Personality Assessment, 45*, 295-300.
Measure: Assertive Job-Hunting Survey (AJHS)
Source: Becker, H. A. (1980). The assertive job-hunting survey. *Measurement and Evaluation in Guidance, 13*, 43-48.
Measure: Generalized Expectancy for Success Scale
Source: Fibel, B., & Hale, W. D. (1978). The generalized expectancy for success scale: A new measure. *Journal of Consulting and Clinical Psychology, 46*, 924-931.

SOURCES OF SELECTED STANDARDIZED MEASURES FOR SERVICES TO OLDER PERSONS

Multiple Standardized Measures

Measure: Mental status, functional status, physical status, economic status, and others
Source: Gallo, J. J., Reichel, W., & Anderson, L. (1988). *Handbook of geriatric assessment*. Rockville, MD: Aspen.
Measure: Measures of physical, mental, and social functioning of clients in long-term care
Source: Kane, R. A., & Kane, R. L. (1981). *Assessing the elderly: A practical guide to measurement*. Lexington, MA: D. C. Heath.
Measure: Measures of intellectual functioning, personality, morale and life satisfaction, self-concept, and others
Source: Mangen, D. J., & Peterson, W. A. (Eds.). (1982). *Clinical and social psychology: Research instruments in social gerontology* (Vol. 1). Minneapolis: University of Minnesota Press.
Measure: Socioeconomic status, kinship relations, religiosity, and others
Source: Mangen, D. J., & Peterson, W. A. (Eds.). (1982). *Social roles and social participation: Research instruments in social gerontology* (Vol. 2). Minneapolis: University of Minnesota Press.
Measure: Measures of health and health services use
Source: Mangen, D. J., & Peterson, W. A. (Eds.). (1984). *Health, program evaluation, and demography: Research instruments in social gerontology* (Vol. 3). Minneapolis: University of Minnesota Press.

Standardized Measures for Use in Evaluating Functional Status

Measure: Katz Index of Activities of Daily Living (ADL)

Source: Katz, S., Ford, A. B., & Moskowitz, R. W. (1963). Studies of illness in the aged: The index of ADL. *Journal of the American Medical Association, 185,* 914-919.

Measure: Modified Barthel Index of Activities of Daily Living

Source: Mahoney, F. I., & Barthel, D. W. (1965). Functional evaluation: The Barthel index. *Rehabilitation, 14,* 61-65.

Source: Granger, C. V., Albrecht, G. L., & Hamilton, B. B. (1979). Outcome of comprehensive medical rehabilitation: Measurement by PULSES profile and the Barthel index. *Archives of Physicians Medical Rehabilitation, 60,* 145-154.

Measure: OARS Instrumental Activities of Daily Living Scale

Source: *The Older American Resources and Services (OARS) methodology: Multidimensional functional assessment questionnaire* (2nd ed.). (1978). Durham, NC: Duke University Center on Aging and Human Development.

Measure: The Five-Item Instrumental Activities of Daily Living Screening Questionnaire

Source: Fillenbaum, G. (1985). Screening the elderly: A brief instrumental activities of daily living measure. *Journal of American Geriatrics Society, 33,* 698-706.

Standardized Measures for Use in Evaluating Social Status

Measure: The Family APGAR

Source: Smilkstein G., Ashworth, C., & Montano, D. (1982). Validity and reliability of the family APGAR as a test of family function. *Journal of Family Practice, 15,* 303-311.

Measure: Social Resources Section of OARS

Source: *The Older American Resources and Services (OARS) methodology: Multidimensional functional assessment questionnaire* (2nd ed., pp. 157-162). (1978). Durham, NC: Duke University Center for the Study of Aging and Human Development.

Measure: Caregiver Strain Index

Source: Robinson, B. C. (1983). Validation of a caregiver strain index. *Journal of Gerontology, 38,* 344-348.

Standardized Measures for Use in Evaluating Physical Health

Measure: Cornell Medical Index

Source: Monroe, R. T., Whiskin, F. E., Bonacich, P., & Jewell, W. O., III. (1965). The Cornell medical index questionnaire as a measure of health in older people. *Journal of Gerontology, 20,* 18-22.

Measure: OARS Physical Health

Source: *The Older American Resources and Services (OARS) methodology: Multidimensional functional assessment questionnaire* (2nd ed.). (1978). Durham, NC: Duke University Center for the Study of Aging and Human Development.

Chapter 9

LEVEL OF FUNCTIONING SCALES

INTRODUCTION

Some human service programs may require outcome performance measures that capture varying degrees of client quality-of-life changes yet may find that no standardized measure exists. Standardized measures have not been developed for all client quality-of-life changes that are of concern to human service programs. Many of the standardized measures that do exist may also be inappropriate for use with certain client populations. For example, a standardized measure designed for use with adults may be inappropriate for use with juveniles. Some standardized measures may be "culture bound" and thus inappropriate for use with certain ethnic populations and perhaps with recent immigrants. Finally, some human service programs may simply prefer to develop outcome performance measures that capture the functioning levels of clients before and after treatment. In the situations described above, human service programs may want to consider the use of Level of Functioning (LOF) scales.

WHAT ARE LOF SCALES?

LOF scales are a relatively recent development in outcome performance measurement in the human services. Although LOF scales have been defined in the literature more by example than by formal definition (Kettner et al., 1990; Kuechler et al., 1988), they can be operationally defined as a before-and-after client assessment instrument designed for use with a particular human service program that attempts to capture an important dimension of client functioning. Client functioning is broadly defined to

TABLE 9.1 Level of Functioning Scales for Use in a Congregate Meals Program for Older Persons

	Circle the Most Appropriate Response				
1. Physical appearance	1	2	3	4	5

Level 1: Lack of concern or awareness of physical appearance; personal hygiene and clothing neglected
Level 3: Verbalizes concern about appearance; some assistance required
Level 5: Careful attention to appearance and personal hygiene

2. Consumption of meals	1	2	3	4	5

Level 1: Consumes ⅓ or less of meal provided
Level 3: Consumes approximately ½ of meal provided
Level 5: Consistently consumes entire meal; may request seconds

3. Weight	1	2	3	4	5

Level 1: Grossly overweight or underweight according to ideal weight for age and body type
Level 3: Overweight or underweight but motivated to change condition
Level 5: Maintaining appropriate weight for age and body type

include not only functioning but also behaviors and problems. Some LOF scales are designed for use with specific client populations, whereas others expand the definition of client to include the client's family.

LOF scales share several common features. As a general rule, each LOF scale is concerned with only one aspect, or dimension, of client functioning. For example, one LOF scale might deal with the social adjustment of juvenile clients, another with alcohol and drug abuse, and yet another with school attendance. For this reason, LOF scales are generally used in combinations. LOF scales dealing with social adjustment, alcohol and drug abuse, and school attendance might be used to develop a composite profile of juvenile clients. Table 9.1 illustrates another example of three LOF scales that can be used together in a congregate meals program for older persons.

LOF scales are generally ranked from a *very low* to a *very high* level of functioning with at least some of the scale points containing descriptors, or descriptive statements. Some LOF scales, such as those shown in Table 9.1, use descriptors at both end points and at the midpoint. The person completing the scale uses the points without descriptors (points 2 and 4) to locate clients who fall between the points with descriptors.

LOF scales are usually administered to clients at entry into a human service program and again on completion of treatment or the receipt of a full complement of services. LOF scales, like standardized measures, are administered in this before-and-after fashion to create a baseline profile of a client at entry into a human service program and a treatment profile (intermediate outcome performance measure) or a posttreatment profile (ultimate outcome performance measure) on completion of treatment or the receipt of a full complement of services.

PRINCIPLES IN DESIGNING LOF SCALES

The principles that apply to designing good measurement instruments also apply to designing LOF scales (Babbie, 1992; Rossi & Freeman, 1993). These principles are discussed in the following sections under the headings of (a) developing a conceptual framework, (b) developing descriptors, (c) respondent considerations, and (d) constructing LOF scales.

DEVELOPING A CONCEPTUAL FRAMEWORK

Well-designed LOF scales are rooted in a knowledge of theory, research, and practice about a human service program and the client population served (Labaw, 1980). Any time clients are observed and rated, it is important that the *dimensions of functioning* on which the rating is based and the *descriptors* used to anchor the points on the scale be based on an understanding of the program, the client population served, and the social problem. In rating the functioning of children in a day care program, for example, a casual observer might be tempted to construct LOF scales that focus exclusively on disruptive and acting-out behavior. A knowledge of child behavior, however, would make it readily evident that the withdrawn and quiet child who displays little affect may well depict the more serious problem.

Input into the development of LOF scales by program staff, administrators, and other stakeholders (e.g., citizens, funding sources, advocacy groups, etc.) is important but is no substitute for a sound knowledge of the theoretical, research, and practice literature. Table 9.2 illustrates three LOF scales for use in an adult day care program that demonstrate the incorporation of a theoretical and research-based understanding of the social and interpersonal behaviors important to older clients.

DEVELOPING DESCRIPTORS

There are three important considerations in the development of descriptors for LOF scales. First, they should describe observable dimensions of client functioning. Second, they should discriminate between different levels of client functioning. Third, they should ideally reflect client behaviors (Labaw, 1980).

TABLE 9.2 Level of Functioning Scales Used to Rate Interactive Behaviors in an Adult
Day Care Program

Circle the Most Appropriate Response

1. Socialization   1   2   3   4   5
   Level 1: Is withdrawn; stays alone; neither voluntarily talks to or interacts with staff or
            other clients; demonstrates no interest in any interpersonal relationships
   Level 3: Must be encouraged to interact with staff or other clients; demonstrates mini-
            mal interest in interpersonal relationships
   Level 5: Is outgoing and skillful at building relationships with staff and other clients
2. Participation   1   2   3   4   5
   Level 1: No participation in activities provided for clients; refuses to participate under
            any circumstances
   Level 3: Will participate in activities with encouragement
   Level 5: Actively participates and encourages others
3. Conversation   1   2   3   4   5
   Level 1: Does not initiate or respond to any conversation with other clients or staff
   Level 3: Expresses desire to talk with others but engages in limited verbal interaction
   Level 5: Is highly conversant and enjoys talking with other clients and staff

Each descriptor used in an LOF scale should describe a particular level of client functioning that can be determined through direct observation. Descriptors should also be written using simple, unambiguous, and verifiable statements. Respondents who complete LOF scales should not be expected to speculate about a client's level of functioning. The LOF scales depicted in Table 9.3 provide examples of the use of simple, straightforward language.

Another important consideration in the development of LOF scales is accuracy. A typical LOF scale will contain points that range across a wide spectrum of client functioning, from severely problematic to great strength and stability. Within this range, LOF scale points should allow for as accurate a depiction of each *individual* client as possible, yet at the same time they should also produce relatively homogeneous *groupings*. For example, if a score of "1" on the LOF scale describing the nutritional status of older clients reflects poor nutrition (i.e., the client is experiencing serious weight loss and/or suffers from obvious nutritional deficits), then all older clients who receive a score of "1" should have about the same level of nutritional deficits. One should not expect to find older clients who fail to maintain a balanced diet but who are otherwise basically healthy included among those who score a "1" on the LOF scale. Table 9.4 depicts an LOF scale that attempts to scale descriptors on the dimension of social adjustment functioning among juvenile first offenders in such a way as to clearly delineate three distinct groups (Levels 1, 3, and 5).

TABLE 9.3 An Example of the Use of Descriptive Language in the Construction of a
Level of Functioning Scale

	Circle the Most Appropriate Response				
1. Household maintenance skills	1	2	3	4	5

Level 1: Basic household maintenance functions such as shopping, budgeting, doing
dishes, making meals, doing laundry and house cleaning are not planned or
managed at all—simply left to be done by the person who is faced with the
need or crisis.

Level 3: Some basic household maintenance functions are assigned and carried out, but
many are left unassigned and undone. The resulting disruption acts as a barrier
to independent functioning.

Level 5: Household functions are planned, managed, and carried out. The ability to han-
dle household maintenance functions is a family strength.

TABLE 9.4 The Use of Descriptors to Define Distinctive Groupings in a Level of
Functioning Scale

	Circle the Most Appropriate Response				
1. Social adjustment for juvenile offenders	1	2	3	4	5

Level 1: Juvenile is withdrawn, verbally combative, or disruptive. Behaviors and social
skills pose a definite barrier to success in school or on the job, for even minimum wage employment. In the case of a juvenile who is legally too young to be
employed, current behaviors and social skills are clearly a barrier to future
employment prospects.

Level 3: Juvenile is able to converse at a minimally acceptable level, usually short or
one-word answers. Juvenile makes some attempt to be responsive to others, has
some social skills, and demonstrates a desire to improve.

Level 5: Juvenile is talkative and personable, has good social skills, is accepted by or
even popular with peers, and is considered socially competent or even advanced
for her or his age by adults.

To the extent possible, LOF descriptors should be behaviorally oriented.
For example, if an LOF scale is used to assess clients on the level of family
harmony/discord, the designers of the scale might be tempted to use a term
such as *dysfunctional* as a descriptor. The individuals who actually complete the scales, however, may differ in their interpretation of the meaning
of dysfunctional. Consequently, it is preferable to describe behaviors, such
as the number of arguments or disagreements per day, or the methods used
to resolve disagreements. This point can be illustrated by referring back to
Table 9.1. The LOF scale dealing with consumption of meals in Table 9.1

is more precise than the LOF scale dealing with weight because the former relies exclusively on behavioral referents, whereas the latter requires a working knowledge of age- and height-appropriate weights. Behaviorally oriented descriptors remove the need to make evaluative judgments or interpretations and thus increase reliability. As a general rule, the fewer the number of adjectives used in a descriptor, the more consistent will be the meaning attributed to the descriptor.

RESPONDENT CONSIDERATIONS

Well-designed LOF scales should be written with the respondent in mind (Epstein & Tripodi, 1977). The term *respondent* generally refers to a person who provides information about him- or herself. In the case of LOF scales, however, the term *respondent* typically refers to a professional staff member who completes the scales on the basis of knowledge and direct observation of a client.

Only three ways exist for a respondent to know something about a client: (a) by observing a client directly, (b) by asking a client about her- or himself, and (c) by getting information about a client from a third party (Nurius & Hudson, 1993). In using LOF scales, particular attention should be paid to the length of time a respondent is expected to know a client before completing the scale, the type and sources of information about the client that are available to the respondent, and the amount of information required by the respondent to make an accurate assessment of the client. For example, if a respondent is attempting to assess a client's level of family harmony/discord, simply asking a client (especially in a first interview) is unlikely to produce an accurate assessment. If time is allowed for the respondent to develop a professional relationship with the client and to meet and become familiar with other family members, the accuracy of the response will probably increase.

In the guidelines for the completion of LOF scales, respondents should be encouraged to make planned, formal observations, either in a client's home, in a natural setting in the community, or in the observer's office. Epstein and Tripodi (1977) propose guidelines for making research-based observations that are useful in thinking about the completion of LOF scales on the basis of direct observation of clients:

What Is to Be Observed? The respondent should be familiar with the LOF scales to be used and should be prepared to focus on a set of expected client behaviors that reflect the areas of functioning under study. If the data are to be gathered through an interview, behavioral referents will be useful in clarifying for the client what is meant by the question.

Site of the Observation. Clients may exhibit different behaviors and give different responses depending on the setting in which the LOF scales are administered. For this reason, respondents should be consistent in the selection of settings for observations. Using multiple settings with the same client may result in differences in observations that have more to do with the setting than with the client.

Frequency of the Observations. In the interest of standardization and reliability, it is important to establish a set number of observations that a respondent uses as a basis for completing an LOF scale. In a residential treatment center, children are generally available for many observations each day. In contrast, couples receiving marriage counseling are typically available once a week for an hour. For the sake of consistency, a set number and type of observations should be specified in the training and preparation of respondents.

Avoiding Influencing the Observation Situation. Objectivity is critical in completing LOF scales. The respondent should make every attempt to be neutral and not influence the observation. Interjecting comments intended to help a client struggle through a difficult part of an interview or to temper feelings such as anger may result in a less accurate observation.

Reliability of the Observation. Whenever possible, a set of procedures should be established for the completion of LOF scales. The purpose of the procedures is to ensure that the administration of LOF scales varies as little as possible between respondents and from client to client. The procedures should include instructions on the expected number and types of observations on which the LOF scales are to be based, the recommended site(s) of the observation(s), what clients can be told about the LOF scales, what the respondent is hoping to accomplish, and other factors that will help to ensure greater uniformity. Respondents should also be reminded of the factors of boredom and fatigue and a tendency to take the procedures for granted through time. The result can be carelessness and a decline in both the reliability of the process and the accuracy of the resulting data.

CONSTRUCTING LOF SCALES

The actual construction of LOF scales should probably be carried out by a small group. As with the development of any performance measure, the process of developing LOF scales should involve stakeholders. All the group members, however, should be knowledgeable about the human service program, the client population served, and the social problem the program addresses. The actual development of LOF scales often requires multiple preliminary drafts, thereby affording ample opportunity for feedback, changes, additions, deletions, and corrections. The following steps are typically used to produce good usable LOF scales:

Step 1: Select the Functions to Be Rated

This is a crucial step because the functions selected form the basis for what will eventually become the outcome performance measures for the human service program. All the functions identified should be capable of changing as the result of a client participating in the human service program.

At this step, it is also necessary to ensure that each identified function is separate and distinct from the others and that no individual function is made up of multiple dimensions. For example, many congregate meals programs for older persons have two major components, a nutrition component and a socialization and recreation component. But these components represent two distinct functions. Consequently, it would be inappropriate to develop an LOF scale that attempts to measure both socialization and recreation. The preferable approach would be to create at least two separate LOF scales, one dealing with each function.

Step 2: Select the Number of Points on the Scale

Typically an odd number of points is selected to ensure a high point, a low point, and a midpoint. The midpoint on an LOF scale can be described as that precarious balancing point at which the client can go either way. With appropriate and timely intervention, the client may show improvement. With neglect, the client may deteriorate.

Some LOF scales have 5 points, others 7 points, and still others as many as 12 points. At a minimum, an LOF scale needs at least 3 points to provide sufficient variability for measurement purposes. Conversely, LOF scales with more than 9 points may provide too much variability, thereby reducing interrater reliability.

Step 3: Write the Descriptors

Descriptors should be based on typical, observable, verifiable client behaviors. For descriptors to be useful across many hundreds—or even thousands—of clients, it may be necessary to describe several types of functioning at each level. For example, a residential treatment center for adolescents attempting to assess expression of affection used several different descriptors to identify *Level 1,* the low point on the scale:

a. regularly is unresponsive when someone makes healthy overtures of affection;
b. limits physical interaction with others (touching) to hitting, poking, or pinching—typically negative, hostile gestures;
c. consistently expresses affection in an unhealthy, sexual manner;
d. is unable to express affection to same-sex peers in an acceptable age-appropriate manner;
e. regularly expresses romantic feelings toward the opposite sex in a blatantly unacceptable, overly sexual manner.

Step 4: Field-Test the LOF Scales

Once good working drafts of the LOF scales to be used in a human service program have been developed, they should be circulated among staff members for use in field testing with clients. On the basis of the field test, staff suggestions, additions, deletions, and corrections are incorporated. Final working drafts of LOF scales are then ready for reliability testing.

Step 5: Test Reliability of the LOF Scales

Reliability testing involves several respondents completing the LOF scales for the same clients. Case scenarios can be used either in written form, on video, or in a role-play simulation. A simple index of interrater reliability can then be computed on the basis of the percentage of agreements. An index of 70% to 80% interrater agreement is generally regarded as fairly high (Epstein & Tripodi, 1977).

A CASE EXAMPLE: LOF SCALES
IN A CHILD RESIDENTIAL TREATMENT CENTER

This case example involves an actual residential treatment center for children (the human service program) providing a program of services including congregate living, education, psychosocial therapy, recreation, and others. A constant concern of the program staff was consistency of treatment planning and intervention. The therapists, however, often observed and treated one set of behaviors, the teachers another, and the residential staff yet another. The different perspectives and treatments contributed to an inconsistent environment for the children, precisely the opposite of what most of them needed.

To remedy the situation, the executive director launched a project to develop a set of LOF scales and to use them as the basis for establishing consistency of assessment and treatment as well as serving as client outcome performance measures. The effort was supported by a faculty person and a student intern from a local school of social work. In the first phase, a review of the literature was conducted to identify behaviors exhibited by adolescents. An extensive list of behaviors was compiled. The list was subsequently reduced through a series of reviews with professional staff and other stakeholders and an exploration of additional literature. Ultimately, LOF scales were developed for 10 behaviors:

1. Quality of verbal interaction
2. Verbal expression of anger
3. Physical expression of anger
4. Expression of affection
5. Affect
6. Level of socialization
7. Regard for rules and conduct
8. Treatment of property
9. Attention to personal health and hygiene
10. Use of drugs and/or medication

A 9-point scale was selected. Point 1 was to be used in describing the expression of a behavior at an extreme level of social unacceptability. Point 9 was to be used to describe the behavior in model or ideal age-appropriate terms. Point 9 was intended to depict a level of socially acceptable behavior that is rarely achieved. Point 5 was used to define the midpoint of demarcation when a behavior and its intensity, frequency, time, place of occurrence, or all of the foregoing are at a minimally socially acceptable level. Point 5 was to be used to describe the precarious balance between positive and negative behaviors at which intervention could move the behavior toward the positive end of the scale and at which neglect might move the behavior to the negative end of the scale.

The LOF scales were then used to develop baseline profiles of client behaviors within 30 days of client admission. A minimum of two and a maximum of four target behaviors were selected for attention for each child. In this way, staff members could be more consistent in what behaviors were attended to and the ways in which different behaviors were treated. The LOF scales were administered again on completion of treatment or receipt of a full complement of services to asses treatment effects and/or posttreatment effects. In the aggregate, the data from the LOF scales served to improve program planning and delivery by identifying the behaviors most in need of treatment and by providing outcome performance measurement data on how each child responded to the treatment provided.

TABLE 9.5 An Assessment of Level of Functioning Scales as an Outcome Performance
Measure

• Utility	Low to high
• Validity	Medium to high
• Reliability	Medium to high
• Precision	Medium
• Feasibility	Low
• Cost	High
• Unit cost reporting	Low

TRANSLATING LOF
SCALES INTO NUMERIC COUNTS

Because performance measurement uses programs as its unit of analysis, LOF scale data—like those produced by standardized measures—must be translated into numeric counts for reporting purposes. The same process used for standardized measures can be used for LOF scales. Clients can be thought of as falling into two groups, (a) those demonstrating improvement and (b) other. Through the use of this approach, numeric count data can be collected, aggregated, and reported using such categories as (a) the number of clients demonstrating improvement and (b) the proportion of clients demonstrating improvement to the total number of clients who complete treatment or receive a full complement of services.

Fewer options exist in translating LOF scales into numeric counts than exist for standardized measures. This is because LOF scales generally do not have either clinical cutting points or target levels of improvement.

AN ASSESSMENT OF LOF SCALES

Table 9.5 provides a summary assessment of LOF scales. Again, the seven criteria of utility, validity, reliability, precision, feasibility, cost, and unit cost reporting ability are used.

The *utility* of LOF scales as an outcome performance measure is rated as *low* to *high*. Like standardized measures, LOF scales have *high* utility for some stakeholders such as program staff and agency administrators but *low* utility for other stakeholders (e.g., citizens, elected officials, and funding sources) who may be unfamiliar with their use, scoring, and interpretation.

The *validity* of LOF scales is rated as *medium* to *high*. Well-designed LOF scales should measure what they purport to measure. Consequently, face validity should be high. Validity can be enhanced through time by the systematic verification that each descriptor used on an LOF scale measures what it purports to measure.

The *reliability* of LOF scales is rated as *medium* to *high*. LOF scales can be continuously tested and modified to increase both interrater and intrarater reliability. As scales are used through time and staff become more experienced in making judgments about level of client functioning, reliability is typically increased (Epstein & Tripodi, 1977; Kuechler et al., 1988).

The *precision* of LOF scales is rated as *medium*. Although LOF scales are more precise than numerical counts, they tend to be less precise than standardized measures. If precision is a priority concern, additional points and descriptors can be added to LOF scales. A point of diminishing utility is reached, however, at which additional points and descriptors add little to the precision of LOF scales.

The *feasibility* of LOF scales is rated as *low*. The use of LOF scales—like standardized measures—requires a considerable commitment of staff, time, and money. Program staff may also find the complexity of LOF scales intrusive, a problem that can hinder their use.

The *cost* of LOF scales is rated as *high*. Costs include staff costs, and perhaps consultant time, to develop the LOF scales and additional staff time and costs to assess clients using the LOF scales. In addition, the supervisory, management, and administrative costs involved in collecting, aggregating, and reporting the resulting data can be considerable.

Finally, the *unit cost reporting* ability of LOF scales is rated as *low*. LOF scales suffer from the same problems of interpretation as standardized measures. How does one interpret the following unit cost: $1,200 to move one client one point on a particular LOF scale?

Chapter 10

CLIENT SATISFACTION

INTRODUCTION

The last of the four major types of outcome performance measures to be discussed is client satisfaction. Because much of the introductory groundwork on client satisfaction was presented in Chapter 5 dealing with quality performance measures, the discussion here is considerably abbreviated. This brevity should not be construed as reflecting negatively on the relative importance of client satisfaction as compared with the other three types of outcome performance measures.

USING CLIENT SATISFACTION
AS AN OUTCOME PERFORMANCE MEASURE

In addition to serving as a quality performance measure, as was demonstrated in Chapter 5, client satisfaction can also be used as an outcome performance measure. Client satisfaction becomes an outcome performance measure when clients are asked to self-report about quality-of-life changes they experienced through participation in human service programs.

The actual process of using client satisfaction as an outcome performance measure is relatively straightforward—provided a human service program already collects and reports quality performance data based on consumer satisfaction surveys. For example, the client satisfaction survey questionnaire shown in Table 5.5 could be used to generate outcome performance measures data by *simply adding one additional question.*

Continuing with the previous examples (information and referral, home-delivered meals, and counseling), Table 10.1 demonstrates how one additional

TABLE 10.1 Using a Client Satisfaction Survey to Generate Outcome Performance Measurement Data

Information and Referral
    Question: Has the information and referral program been helpful to you in accessing needed services?

Not at All Helpful				Very Helpful
1	2	3	4	5

Home-Delivered Meals
    Question: Has the home-delivered meals program been helpful to you in maintaining your health and nutrition?

Not at All Helpful				Very Helpful
1	2	3	4	5

Counseling
    Question: Has the counseling program been helpful to you in coping with the stress in your life?

Not at All Helpful				Very Helpful
1	2	3	4	5

client satisfaction question on a survey can generate outcome performance measures data for each of these three human service programs. Because these three questions ask clients to self-report on quality-of-life changes, the questions become outcome performance measures and the resulting client responses constitute outcome performance measures data.

TRANSLATING CLIENT SATISFACTION OUTCOMES INTO NUMERIC COUNTS

Because of the preference of governments at all levels for numeric counts as outcome performance measures, some thought needs to be given to how client satisfaction outcome data can be translated into numeric counts. Fortunately, this process is not difficult. One approach (see Table 10.1) is to simply determine the actual number, or percentage, of clients responding *very helpful* to each question. The resulting numeric counts might look something like this:

- 78% of responding clients rate the information and referral program as *very helpful* in accessing needed services.
- 82% of responding clients rate the home-delivered meals program as *very helpful* in enabling them to maintain their health and nutrition.
- 55% of responding clients report that the counseling program was *very helpful* in coping with stress in their lives.

TABLE 10.2   Assessment of Client Satisfaction as an Outcome Performance Measure

• Utility	Medium
• Validity	Low to medium
• Reliability	Medium
• Precision	Low
• Feasibility	Medium
• Cost	Low to high for start-up
• Unit cost reporting	High

AN ASSESSMENT
OF CLIENT SATISFACTION

Table 10.2 summarizes the assessment of using client satisfaction as an outcome performance measure. The rating criteria of utility, validity, reliability, precision, feasibility, cost, and unit cost reporting are discussed below.

The *utility* of using client satisfaction as an outcome performance measure is rated as *medium.* Client satisfaction is of interest to a variety of stakeholders. Elected officials, funding agencies (government and foundations), program administrators, and agency administrators are all generally interested in—and concerned about—clients' perceptions of the effectiveness of human service programs. Most stakeholders also recognize the inherent limitations of client satisfaction data.

The *validity* of using client satisfaction as an outcome performance measure is rated as *low* to *medium.* Client satisfaction by its very nature is subjective, and many clients are "involuntary." One can never be sure that clients' assessments of quality-of-life changes are accurate. Nevertheless, clients provide an important perspective on the effectiveness of human service programs that cannot be gained from any of the other three types of outcome performance measures.

The *reliability* of using client satisfaction as an outcome performance measure is rated as *medium.* Reliability as it pertains to the use of client satisfaction as an outcome measure is related primarily to the degree of variability in the survey questions used to solicit the data. Reliability can be enhanced by using standardized survey questions that do not vary from client to client or from survey to survey.

The *precision* of using client satisfaction as an outcome performance measure is rated as *low.* Client self-reporting by its very nature is not precise. Asking clients to self-report on their quality-of-life changes incurred as a result of having participated in human service programs is perhaps even less precise.

TABLE 10.3 An Assessment of the Four Types of Outcome Performance Measures

Criterion	Numeric Counts	Standardized Measures	LOF Scales	Client Satisfaction
Utility	High	Low to high	Low to high	Medium
Validity	Low to medium	High	Medium to high	Low to medium
Reliability	High	High	Medium to high	Medium
Precision	Low	Medium to high	Medium	Low
Feasibility	High	Low	Low	Medium
Cost	Low to medium	High	High	Low to high
Unit cost reporting	High	Low	Low	High

The *feasibility* of using client satisfaction as an outcome performance measure is rated as *medium*. Although the process of actually collecting data can be cumbersome, the effort required is probably no greater than that required for the other types of outcome performance measures. A caveat here is that feasibility probably declines with time. Tracking down and surveying clients months after they have completed treatment or have received a full complement of services is problematic.

The *cost* of using client satisfaction as an outcome performance measure ranges from *low* to *high*. If a human service program is already collecting client satisfaction data to serve as a quality performance measure, the incremental cost of adding, analyzing, and reporting data on one additional question—or even a few additional questions—should be *low*. If client satisfaction data are not currently collected, start-up costs including the cost of developing the surveys, surveying clients, and analyzing and reporting the data will probably be *high*.

The *unit cost reporting* ability of using client satisfaction as an outcome performance measure is rated as *high*. Outcome performance measures data based on client satisfaction will closely resemble numeric counts (i.e., a specified number or percentage of clients achieving a quality-of-life change).

AN ASSESSMENT OF THE FOUR TYPES
OF OUTCOME PERFORMANCE MEASURES

Now that all four types of outcome performance measures have been introduced and discussed, it may be useful to compare and contrast them using the common criteria of utility, validity, reliability, precision, feasibility, cost, and unit cost reporting ability. As Table 10.3 illustrates, each of the four types of outcome performance measures has advantages and disadvantages. For example, standardized measures and LOF scales are rated as more precise, valid, and reliable, but they are also rated as costing more. Numeric counts are considered as having more utility and costing less, but they also are considered to be less valid, reliable, and precise. Client satisfaction, by comparison, is more middle-of-the-road, rated *medium* on more criteria than any of the other three.

In the final analysis, it is probably the nature of the human service program itself and the preferences of stakeholders that may ultimately determine which type or types of outcome performance measures are used. Many human service programs may wind up using at least two types, numeric counts and one of the other three.

Chapter 11

ISSUES IN SELECTING, COLLECTING, REPORTING, AND USING PERFORMANCE MEASURES

INTRODUCTION

This final chapter discusses some of the major issues and challenges associated with the selection, collection, reporting, and use of performance measurement data to assess and improve the efficiency, quality, and effectiveness of human service programs.

ISSUES IN SELECTING PERFORMANCE MEASURES

As departments of the federal government move to implement the Government Performance and Results Act (1993), some recurring problems are identified in how program administrators—both human services and nonhuman services—go about the process of selecting performance measures (Hatry & Wholey, 1994). The implications of these recurring problems have import not only for the Government Performance and Results Act but also for performance measurement in general. By recognizing these problems—or pitfalls—up front, other human service programs may be able to avoid them in the future and select better performance measures. Four of the more important recurring problems experienced by federal programs in selecting performance measures are:

1. failing to relate performance measures to a program's mission,
2. relying too heavily on existing data,

3. excluding stakeholders from the process, and
4. selecting too few quality performance measures.

FAILING TO RELATE PERFORMANCE MEASURES TO PROGRAM MISSION

Many performance measures relate only tangentially to a program's mission, goals, and objectives. Performance measures should always be directly related to the social problem the program addresses. A good fit between a human service program and its mission, goals, and objectives can be achieved only by staying fixed on the social problem that the program addresses and on the assumptions made about the social problem.

RELYING TOO HEAVILY ON EXISTING DATA

Basing performance measures on existing data is not necessarily a problem, but a problem can arise when the feasibility and cost advantages of using existing data drive out other considerations such as (a) usefulness, (b) validity, (c) reliability, and (d) unit cost reporting. The problem of relying too heavily on existing data can be avoided by subjecting all proposed performance measures to the strict application of the evaluative criteria identified in Chapter 6.

EXCLUDING STAKEHOLDERS FROM THE PROCESS

In balancing the time needed to solicit widespread stakeholder input into the selection of performance measures for a human service program against other, more pressing day-to-day administrative demands, a tendency appears to exist to sacrifice input for time. The result, and the resulting problem, is the adoption of performance measures that stakeholders do not find useful. The solution to avoiding this problem is to involve stakeholders throughout the selection process. It should be noted, however, that there is nothing wrong with demanding quick turnaround time for stakeholder input.

SELECTING TOO FEW QUALITY PERFORMANCE MEASURES

This problem appears specifically related to the absence of client stakeholder input during the selection of performance measures. Without the specific involvement of client stakeholders in the selection process, the client perspective—and, consequently, the quality perspective—appears to get lost. The solution to avoiding this problem is obvious: involve clients.

ISSUES IN REPORTING
PERFORMANCE MEASUREMENT DATA

In discussing the reporting of performance measurement data, three questions arise.

1. How often should performance measurement data be reported?
2. How much time does it take to collect and aggregate performance measurement data?
3. How should performance measurement data be displayed?

THE FREQUENCY OF
PERFORMANCE MEASUREMENT REPORTING

The frequency of performance measurement reporting ultimately depends on how the data are to be used. If the resulting performance measurement data are to be used primarily to assess the efficiency, quality, and effectiveness of human service programs and/or to satisfy reporting requirement, then annual reporting is sufficient. The annual reporting of performance measurement data should satisfy most reporting requirements such as SEA reporting and the Government Performance and Results Act of 1993, both of which link performance measurement reporting with the annual budget process.

For purposes of effecting program improvements, however, the reporting of performance measurement data on a more frequent basis than annually is generally recommended (e.g., Hatry & Wholey, 1994). More frequent reporting enables program administrators and stakeholders to spot efficiency, quality, and effectiveness problems with human service programs and to take corrective action more quickly than does annual reporting. The concept of quarterly reporting suggests itself, with the possible exception of performance measurements based on client satisfaction data, for which biannual reporting is probably sufficient, assuming a stable program.

THE COST OF COLLECTING
PERFORMANCE MEASUREMENT DATA

Cost is certainly one of the major considerations in determining how frequently to report performance measurement data. A key factor in determining cost is the amount of staff time required to collect and aggregate performance measurement data and the frequency of data collection (e.g., quarterly, biannually, annually).

The city of Portland, Oregon, has been experimenting with performance measurement data using SEA reporting categories since 1991. Portland has also been keeping track of the amount of staff time required to generate the performance measurement data. On average, it takes programs, both human services and nonhuman services, an average of about 10 hours total to collect, aggregate, and report 12 months of performance measurement data one time each year, with a range of 5 to 20 hours (Tracy & Jean, 1993, p. 13). The Portland experience also suggests that the time required to collect performance measurement data declines through time. The learning curve is steep at the beginning, then levels out, and finally dips. Assuming that the Portland experience is not atypical, the staff time and costs associated with quarterly reporting appear to be manageable for most human service programs.

THE DISPLAYING OF
PERFORMANCE MEASUREMENT DATA

No particular format exists for displaying performance measurement data. Human service programs desiring to satisfy the GASB's requirements of SEA reporting, however, will necessarily have to report certain predetermined types of data including inputs, outputs, quality and outcome performance measures, and cost efficiency and cost effectiveness ratios. The reporting format illustrated in Table 11.1 combines the types of data required by SEA reporting with the types of performance measures discussed in this book. Table 11.1, then, can be thought of as a model for reporting performance measurement data on human service programs. Table 11.2 illustrates what the completed reporting format might look like using the data from the family counseling agency example presented in Chapter 2. Both Tables 11.1 and 11.2 present data for multiple time periods. This practice appears to be the norm and is designed to illustrate trends and provide for between-period comparisons.

The initial performance measurement reports developed by most human service programs will probably not look like the model illustrated in Tables 11.1 and 11.2. A more likely scenario is that performance measurement reports will start out reporting some, but not all, of the information shown in the two tables and then gradually through time will move toward approximating the model. An example of what an initial performance measurement report for a human service program might really look like is presented in Table 11.3.

Table 11.3 presents data taken from an early performance measurement report for a job training program operated by the Phoenix Human Resources Department (City of Phoenix, 1992). As one might expect, some performance measurement data are displayed; other data are missing. Service completions and intermediate outcome numeric counts are shown, but

TABLE 11.1 A Model Performance Measurement Reporting Format for Human Service Programs

| | Human Service Program | | |
	1999	2000	2001
I. Inputs			
A. Financial resources (in $)	____	____	____
B. Human resources (in FTEs)	____	____	____
II. Outputs			
A. Intermediate outputs (in time, material, or episode units of service)	____	____	____
B. Final outputs (in service completions)	____	____	____
III. Quality			
A. Client satisfaction (percentage *satisfied* or *very satisfied*)	____	____	____
B. Outputs with quality dimensions (number or percentage of outputs that meet quality specifications)	____	____	____
IV. Outcomes			
A. Intermediate outcomes: Numeric counts (number or percentage of clients who achieve a specified quality-of-life change)	____	____	____
B. Ultimate outcomes: Numeric counts (number or percentage of clients who achieve a specified quality-of-life change)	____	____	____
V. Cost Efficiency Ratios			
A. Cost per intermediate output	____	____	____
B. Intermediate outputs per FTE	____	____	____
C. Cost per final output	____	____	____
D. Final outputs per FTE	____	____	____
VI. Cost Effectiveness Ratios			
A. Cost per intermediate outcome	____	____	____
B. Intermediate outcomes per FTE	____	____	____
C. Cost per ultimate outcome	____	____	____
D. Ultimate outcomes per FTE	____	____	____

intermediate outputs (units of service) and final outcomes are missing. The report acknowledges the importance of quality performance measures by the inclusion of a client satisfaction dimension. Unfortunately, at the time the report was issued, apparently no data were available. The report also includes the total cost of the job training program and the number of total full-time equivalent positions working on the program. Because data on inputs (financial resources) as well as outputs and outcomes are presented, the report could have also included cost efficiency and cost effectiveness ratios—but did not. We calculated the ratios shown.

TABLE 11.2 A Performance Measurement Report for a Family Counseling Program

	Family Counseling Program		
	1999	*2000*	*2001*
I. Inputs			
A. Financial resources (in thousands)	$750	$800	$850
B. Human resources (in FTEs)	22	24	26
II. Outputs			
A. Intermediate outputs			
(hours of counseling service)	27,500	30,000	32,000
B. Final outputs (service completions)	225	250	275
III. Quality			
A. Client satisfaction (percentage			
satisfied or *very satisfied*)	85	87	88
IV. Outcomes			
A. Intermediate (number of clients			
with no child abuse referrals)	112	125	150
V. Cost Efficiency Ratios			
A. Cost per output	$27.27	$26.66	$26.56
B. Outputs per FTE	1,250	1,250	1,231
VI. Cost Effectiveness Ratios			
A. Cost per outcome	$6,696	$6,400	$5,666
B. Outcomes per FTE	5.1	5.2	5.8

ISSUES IN USING
PERFORMANCE MEASUREMENT DATA

The use of performance measurement data to actually improve the efficiency, quality, and effectiveness of human service programs is best examined in two parts. The next sections discuss (a) improving direct program delivery and (b) improving contract program delivery.

IMPROVING DIRECT DELIVERY

How can performance measurement data be used to improve the direct delivery of human service programs? The answer is by analyzing performance measurement data through time and by making comparisons with other programs and with other regions. In contemporary management jargon, this activity is frequently referred to as *benchmarking* (Martin, 1993; Spendolini, 1992).

Table 11.3 illustrates how the analysis of performance measurement data can be used to make program improvements. An analysis of Table 11.3 generates several questions:

TABLE 11.3 An Initial Performance Measures Report for a Human Services Program

	Job Training Program		
	FY89	FY90	FY91
I. Inputs			
1. Financial resources (in thousands)	$8,257	$7,689	$7,033
2. Human resources (in FTEs)	33.50	33.25	33.92
II. Outputs			
1. Service completions	4,388	3,783	3,124
III. Quality			
1. Client satisfaction	N/A	N/A	N/A
IV. Outcomes			
1. Number of placements	902	820	452
V. Cost Efficiency Ratios			
1. Cost per output	$1,882	$2,033	$2,251
2. Outputs per FTE	131	114	92
VI. Cost Effectiveness Ratios			
1. Cost per outcome	$9,154	$9,377	$15,559
2. Outcomes per FTE	27	24.7	13.3

SOURCE: Adapted from City of Phoenix, Arizona (1992).
NOTE: Ratios were not included in the original report.

1. Service completions are down 29% during the 3 years. Why? Is the decline related simply to decreased resources, or are other factors involved?
2. Why have no client satisfaction surveys been conducted? What is being done to remedy this situation?
3. Why are job placements (a numeric count outcome performance measure) down 50% during the 3 years? Clients graduating from the program (service completions) are down only 29%. Is the program training people for jobs that do not exist? Has the economy simply turned bad? Or are other as yet undiscovered factors at work here?
4. Why has the cost effectiveness ratio gone "through the roof"? In fiscal year 1989, the cost per outcome (one job placement) was $9,154; in 1991, the cost was $15,559—an increase of 70%.

Determining the answers to the above questions, as well as others that could be derived from the performance measurement data presented in Table 11.3, should be sufficient to keep a program administrator occupied for several weeks, if not months.

If the job training program has multiple subcomponents, such as an on-the-job-training component and a basic skills training component, the performance measurement data in Table 11.3 could be disaggregated into these two components and each analyzed separately. This process might provide useful insights into the relative efficiency, quality, and effectiveness of the various types of job training. In the same vein, if the job training program had multiple regional site locations, the performance measurement data could be disaggregated and analyzed by region. When differences between subcomponents or regions are discovered, the better-performing subcomponents or regions can be studied to determine why their performance is superior. The lessons learned from such study may be transferable to the other subcomponents or regions.

IMPROVING CONTRACT DELIVERY

Most government human service programs today are operated partially, or totally, via purchase of service contracts (Kettner & Martin, 1994). Human service programs that operate under contracts can improve their efficiency, quality, and effectiveness by (a) requiring contractors to collect and report performance measurement data and (b) adopting performance contracting.

The same output, quality, and outcome performance measures used in direct delivery of a human service program can be used in purchase of service contracts. Contractors can be required to collect and report performance measurement data. The contracting agency can then use the data to compare and contrast the relative efficiency, quality, and effectiveness of its contractors. Relationships can be strengthened with those contractors that perform well, whereas relationships can be reduced, or even terminated, with those contractors that do not perform well.

Once contractors become used to collecting and reporting performance measurement data, a move to performance contracting can be made. Performance contracting can be defined as any purchase of service contract that ties at least a portion of a contractor's compensation to the achievement of performance measures (Kettner & Martin, 1993). The principal contracting approach in the human services is *cost reimbursement* (Kettner & Martin, 1994). Contractors are reimbursed for the costs they incur, usually in accordance with an approved budget, regardless of the volume of service provided, its quality, or its effectiveness. Once contractors become familiar with performance measurement, no reason exists—except perhaps history and tradition within the human services—why cost reimbursement contracting must continue. Instead, a portion, or all, of a contractor's compensation can be tied directly to the achievement of specific performance measures. The contractor gets paid for performance, not simply for providing service. Table 11.4 is an abbreviated illustration of how the compensation and method of payment portion of a purchase of service contract can be restructured to transform it into a performance contract.

TABLE 11.4 Performance Measures and Performance Contracting

1. Output performance measures
   $ _____ per unit of service (time, episode, material)
   $ _____ per final output (service completion)
2. Quality performance measures
   $ _____ for achieving a predetermined level (e.g., 90%) of client satisfaction
   $ _____ per output with a quality dimension
3. Outcome performance measures
   $ _____ per numeric count
   $ _____ per client achieving a score of _____ on a standardized measure
   $ _____ per client achieving a score of _____ on a level of functioning scale
   $ _____ for achieving a predetermined level (e.g., 85%) of client satisfaction

At least one state, Maine, has already taken steps to make performance contracting mandatory. In 1994, the Maine legislature passed a law requiring the state agencies for human services, mental health and mental retardation, and substance abuse to begin moving toward performance contracting on a phased-in schedule. All contracts entered into by these three state human service agencies after July 1, 1998, are to be performance based (Cahill & Costello, undated, p. 1).

DOES PERFORMANCE MEASUREMENT REALLY MAKE A DIFFERENCE?

The acid test for performance measurement may be the assessment of both usefulness and cost. Does performance measurement really contribute to improving the efficiency, quality, and effectiveness of human service programs? Are the benefits worth the costs? Although empirical studies in this area are limited, the few studies identified from the literature suggest that performance measurement does appear to alter *in a positive fashion* the way programs operate. For example,

- More than 80% of top- and middle-level program managers in the Florida Department of Health and Rehabilitative Services said that the use of performance measures was either *very important* or *somewhat important* to the operation of their programs, whereas some 68% said that the benefits of performance measurement exceeded the costs (FHRS, 1986, p. 7).
- Program administrators working with mentally ill and chemically dependent clients in a county human services agency in Minnesota consistently rated the use of performance measures as "worth the effort" (Kuechler et al., 1988, p. 82).

- Program managers involved with SEA reporting in the city of Portland, Oregon, discovered that the use of performance measures creates a demand for even more and better program information and, in particular, for information that can be used to identify warning trends (Tracy & Jean, 1993).

CONCLUSION

Without question, the future continuation, growth, development, or termination of human service programs will depend on the use of performance measures and the generation of performance measurement data. It is our sincere hope that the frameworks and concepts described in this book will make a positive contribution to the creation of sound and useful performance measurement systems for human service programs.

NEW BEGINNINGS RESIDENTIAL TREATMENT CENTER CASE STUDY

The New Beginnings Residential Treatment Center (NBRTC) is a case study designed to illustrate the performance measurement concepts covered in this book. The case study includes exercises to complete an annual performance measures report.

DESCRIPTION OF
THE HUMAN SERVICE PROGRAMS

The NBRTC is a residential treatment center for boys ages 6 through 18. NBRTC operates three human service programs: residential care, counseling, and education. A maximum of 20 boys can be accommodated at NBRTC at any one time. Given its reputation for efficient, high-quality, and effective services, whenever a vacancy occurs at NBRTC, it is usually filled immediately. The average length of a resident's stay at NBRTC is 2 years.

Residential Care

The residential care program includes the provision of shelter, food, clothing, and supervision and all of the activities that occur during the course of daily living, except for counseling and education. The residents at NBRTC live in five cottages, four boys to a cottage. The residential care program operates 24 hours a day, 7 days a week.

Counseling

The counseling program provides individual and group therapy for the residents. Each resident is required to participate in one individual counseling session per week. Individual counseling sessions range from 45 minutes to 1½ hours. Each

TABLE A.1   Annual Performance Measures Report

	Residential Care	Counseling	Education
I. Inputs			
A. Financial resources ($)	___	___	___
B. Human resources (FTEs)	___	___	___
II. Outputs			
A. Intermediate outputs (in units of service)	___	___	___
B. Final outputs (in service completions)	___	___	___
III. Quality			
A. Outputs with quality dimensions (number or percentage)	___	___	___
IV. Outcomes			
A. Ultimate outcomes: Numeric counts	[_____]		
V. Cost Efficiency Ratios			
A. Cost per intermediate output	___	___	___
B. Intermediate outputs per FTE	___	___	___
C. Cost per final output	___	___	___
D. Final outputs per FTE	___	___	___
VI. Cost Effectiveness Ratios			
A. Cost per ultimate outcome	[_____]		
B. Ultimate outcomes per FTE	[_____]		

resident is also required to attend group counseling sessions. Group sessions are composed of five boys each and meet three times per week. Each group session ranges between $1\frac{1}{2}$ and 2 hours in length.

Education

The education program provides elementary and high school level education to the residents.

MANDATED USE OF
PERFORMANCE MEASUREMENT

NBRTC's major funding sources (the state departments of social services, juvenile corrections, and education) have all mandated the collection and reporting of annual performance measurement data. A common format, modeled on SEA reporting, has also been mandated. The reporting format is shown in Table A.1. You will be asked to refer to this table in several of the exercises that follow. You may want to make a copy of this format and keep it handy to avoid flipping back and forth between sections.

The NBRTC has not been involved with performance measurement before. Consequently, the various programs must identify output, quality, and outcome performance measures and establish a process for collecting, aggregating, and reporting the resulting data. You are the director of NBRTC. You must decide—in consultation with your program administrators, funding sources, parents and guardians, residents, and other stakeholders—what types of output, quality, and outcome performance measures the agency's three programs will use. You must also complete the Annual Performance Measures Report shown in Table A.1.

INPUTS

The inputs section of the Annual Performance Measures Report is designed to capture data on (a) the financial resources expended on each human service program in total program costs and (b) the human resources expended on each human service program in full-time equivalent (FTE) staff.

You have developed a program budget for NBRTC and have allocated all direct and indirect costs to each of your three programs. NBRTC has a staff of 25 and a total annual operating budget of $710,000 divided as follows:

- Residential care: 17 FTEs and a budget of $325,000
- Counseling: 4 FTEs, including 2 full-time therapists and one half-time therapist, and a budget of $160,000
- Education: 4 FTEs and a budget of $225,000

Exercise #1

Complete Section I: Inputs, Parts A and B, of the Annual Performance Measures Report for all three human service programs.

OUTPUT PERFORMANCE MEASURES

Output performance measures are divided into two categories:
(a) intermediate and (b) final.

Intermediate Output Performance Measures

In selecting intermediate output performance measures (or units of service), you must decide what is the single "best" unit of service (time, episode, or material) for each of NBRTC's three human service programs. For the residential care program, all three unit of service options (time, episode, or material) are potentially available. Examples of time units include hours, days, weeks, months, and years. An example of an episode unit might be one stay at NBRTC. Examples of material units might be food, clothing, and shelter. The counseling program and the education program are probably restricted to using either time or episode units because a material unit is most likely not applicable.

After defining intermediate output performance measures (units of service) for each of the three programs, you need to determine how many intermediate outputs each program provided during the past year. Because we do not have real program data to work with, an estimate must be made. For our purposes here, we will simply equate the amount of intermediate outputs (units of service) provided with each program's maximum annual capacity. Points to consider in computing each program's maximum number of intermediate outputs (units of service) are as follows:

1. The NBRTC has a maximum capacity of 20 residents at any one time.
2. The residential care program operates 365 days a year.
3. The counseling program has 2.5 counselors. One counselor is capable of providing 10 individual sessions and 6 group sessions a week.
4. The education program operates for 180 days per year.

Exercise #2

Select intermediate output performance measures (units of service) for all three human service programs. Estimate the maximum number of intermediate outputs each program can produce during a year. Complete Section II: Outputs, Part A, of the Annual Performance Measures Report for all three human service programs.

Final Output Performance Measures

Your challenge here lies in determining what constitutes a service completion (completion of treatment or receipt of a full complement of services) for each of the three human service programs operated by NBRTC. For each of the three human service programs, you must define what it is that each resident must accomplish to achieve a service completion. It may be useful to think of a service completion for residential care as a specified time (e.g., 3 months, 6 months, or 1 year). For the counseling program, you might again consider a specified period, or you might specify some minimum number of individual and/or group counseling sessions that each resident must complete. For the education program, you might consider defining a service completion as an episode (e.g., one report card period, one semester, one school year, etc.)

After defining final output performance measures (service completions) for the three human service programs, you need to estimate the number of service completions each program achieved during the past year. Because we do not have real program data, an estimate must again be made. Points to consider in estimating each program's number of service completions are these:

1. The NBRTC has a maximum capacity of 20 residents at any one time.
2. You should not expect the three programs to be perfect, so some margin of error should be provided. For computational purposes, you might consider computing the maximum number of final outputs each program can produce during 1 year and taking 90% of this number.

Exercise #3

Complete Section II: Outputs, Part B, of the Annual Performance Measures Report for all three human service programs.

QUALITY PERFORMANCE MEASURES

Two types of quality performance measures exist: (a) outputs with quality dimensions and (b) client satisfaction. As the director of NBRTC, you have decided to use outputs with quality dimensions. The other option, client satisfaction, was considered but rejected because of the validity concerns when dealing with clients (residents) who may be placed in treatment against their will. In adopting the outputs with quality dimensions approach, you followed the recommended steps:

Step 1

Select the quality dimensions to be used.
You selected reliability and responsiveness.

Step 2

Relate the quality dimensions to specific characteristics of the individual human service program.
You have related the quality dimensions of reliability and responsiveness to the agency's three human service programs in the following manner:

	Reliability	*Responsiveness*
Residential care	Consistent treatment for compliance and noncompliance with assigned activities	Requests for exceptions to assigned activities are dealt with within 1 hour
Counseling	Assigned counselor conducts sessions	Counseling sessions start on time (within 10 minutes of schedule)
Education	Consistent treatment of acceptable and unacceptable performance	All classes meet as scheduled

Step 3

Graft quality dimensions to intermediate output performance measures.
You have grafted the quality dimensions as follows:

	Reliability	*Responsiveness*
Residential care	One child care day with consistency of treatment	One child care day with timely resolution of exceptions
Counseling	One session with counselor of record	One session starting on time
Education	One school day with consistency of treatment	One school day with all classes meeting as scheduled

You now need to estimate the number of outputs with quality dimensions that each of the three human service programs produced during the past year. Points to consider in estimating each program's number of outputs with quality dimensions are these:

1. If all three human service programs achieved a 100% quality rating, then the number of outputs with quality dimensions provided by each program would be the same as the number of each program's intermediate outputs (units of service).
2. You should not expect the three programs to be perfect, so some margin of error should again be provided. For computational purposes, you might again consider computing the number of outputs with quality dimensions at the rate of 90% of each program's number of intermediate outputs (the numbers you entered in Section II: Outputs, Part A, of the Annual Performance Measures Report).

Exercise #4

Estimate the number of outputs with quality dimensions each human service program achieved last year. *Remember,* this number should be 90% of each human service program's number of intermediate outputs (units of service). Complete Section III: Quality, Part B, of the Annual Performance Measures Report for all three programs.

OUTCOMES

Because the mandated Annual Performance Measures Report does not distinguish between intermediate and ultimate outcomes, your program managers and you have decided to report only on ultimate outcomes. Furthermore, your program administrators and you have decided to establish one common numeric count that will serve as an ultimate outcome performance measure for all three programs. You arrived at this decision because of your conclusion that the NBRTC actually provides a program of services addressing multiproblem male juveniles and that although each program has a specific focus when the clients are in residency, all three programs have a common ultimate goal relating to postplacement adjustment.

Points to consider in estimating NBRTC's number of ultimate outcomes for 1 year are these:

1. On average, 10 residents leave NBRTC each year.

2. You should not expect the residential experience provided by NBRTC to achieve positive results with the residents 100% of the time. For computational purposes, you might consider computing the total number of ultimate outcomes that NBRTC could produce in 1 year and taking 80% of this number.

Exercise #5

Develop a numeric count that you believe can serve as an ultimate outcome performance measure for all three programs. The numeric count should reflect the concept of overall adjustment to postresidential living. Estimate the number of ultimate outcomes that the three human service programs operated by NBRTC—in combination—achieved during the past year. Finally, complete Section IV: Outcome, Part A, of the Annual Performance Measures Report for all three human service programs. *Remember,* you are using a combined numeric count ultimate outcome performance measure for all three programs.

COST EFFICIENCY/COST
EFFECTIVENESS RATIOS

The final step in completing the Annual Performance Measures Report is for you to compute the cost efficiency and cost effectiveness ratios. First, refer to Sections I and II of the Annual Performance Measures Report to get the figures needed to calculate cost per output and outputs per FTE. Second, refer to Sections I and IV-A to get the figures needed to calculate cost per ultimate outcome and ultimate outcomes per FTE. Because you have decided to use one common ultimate outcome performance measure, you will need to aggregate the total financial resources (total program costs) for all three programs and the total FTEs for all three programs.

Exercise #6

Complete Section V: Cost Efficiency Ratios on the Annual Performance Measures Report for all three human service programs.

Exercise #7

Complete Section VI: Cost Effectiveness Ratios on the Annual Performance Measures Report for all three human service programs. *Remember,* you are using a combined numeric count ultimate outcome performance measure for all three human service programs.

Appendix B

ANSWERS TO EXERCISES FROM NEW BEGINNINGS RESIDENTIAL TREATMENT CENTER CASE STUDY

You are encouraged to work through the exercises in Appendix A and develop answers independently. In the event that you do not understand an exercise or the framework for considering the exercise, the following suggested responses are provided. A certain amount of creativity is required in the development of performance measures. Consequently, in several instances (e.g., intermediate and final outputs, ultimate outcomes, and cost efficiency and cost effectiveness ratios), the answers provided should not be considered as the only correct ones.

Exercise #1

1. Complete Section I: Inputs, Parts A and B, of the Annual Performance Measures Report for all three human service programs.
   The answers are as follows:

	Residential Care	*Counseling*	*Education*
A. Financial resources	$325,000	$160,000	$225,000
B. Human resources (FTEs)	17	4	4

Exercise #2

1. Select intermediate output performance measures for all three human service programs.
2. Estimate the maximum number of intermediate outputs each program can produce during a year.
3. Complete Section II: Outputs, Part A, of the Annual Performance Measures Report for all three human service programs.

RESIDENTIAL CARE

In the residential care program, the most useful intermediate output (unit of service) is probably one child care day, defined as one resident in the care of the NBRTC for one 24-hour period. Because NBRTC has a capacity of 20 residents at any one time, the maximum number of intermediate outputs (units of service) that the program can produce in 1 year is 7,300 (20 residents × 365 days).

COUNSELING

Individual counseling sessions range from 45 minutes to $1\frac{1}{2}$ hours, whereas the group sessions range from $1\frac{1}{2}$ to 2 hours. Each resident participates in one individual and three group sessions per week. The counseling program could define an intermediate output (unit of service) using either (a) a time increment (perhaps 15 minutes to allow for the differences in the length of sessions) or (b) an episode unit defined as one session. Unless some overriding reason exists for using a time unit, the preferable choice here is probably to use the episode unit.

Two full-time and one half-time counselors work in the counseling program. One full-time counselor is capable of providing 10 individual sessions and 6 group sessions per week for a total of 16 sessions per week. Consequently, the maximum number of intermediate outputs (units of service) the counseling program can produce in 1 year is 2,080 (2.5 counselors × 16 sessions per week × 52 weeks).

EDUCATION

The education program might use a child school day, defined as one child in attendance for at least 4 hours, as an intermediate output (unit of service). Because the maximum resident capacity of NBRTC is 20 residents at any one time and the education program runs for 180 days, the maximum number of intermediate outputs (units of service) the program can produce in 1 year is 3,600 (20 residents × 180 days).

Exercise #3

1. Define a final output performance measure (service completion) for each of the three human service programs.
2. Estimate the number of final outputs (service completions) each human service program achieved during the year.

3. Complete Section II: Outputs, Part B, of the Annual Performance Measures Report for all three human service programs.

RESIDENTIAL CARE

The residential care program might define a final output (service completion) as one resident completing at least 75 child care days during a fiscal quarter (i.e., a 3-month period) while participating in at least 80% of assigned activities. This approach has the advantages of (a) establishing a minimum number of days that each resident must be in care, (b) specifying a minimum proportion of assigned activities that each resident must accomplish, and (c) creating a reasonable time frame (3 months) for purposes of calculating a final output or service completion. Because the maximum resident capacity of NBRTC is 20 residents at any one time, the maximum number of final outputs (service completions) that the residential care program can produce in 1 year is 80 (20 residents × 4 fiscal quarters). Any number of final outputs (service completions) up to and including 80, then, is theoretically possible. For purposes of estimating the number of service completions for 1 year, a 90% rate is used, which translates into 72 final outputs (service completions) for the residential care program for 1 year (80 × 0.9).

COUNSELING

The counseling program might define a final output (service completion) as one resident participating in at least 80% of the required individual and group therapy sessions during a fiscal quarter (i.e., a 3-month period). Because the resident capacity of NBRTC is 20 residents at any one time, the maximum number of final outputs (service completions) that can be produced by the counseling program in 1 year is again 80 (20 residents × 4 fiscal quarters). Any number of final outputs (service completions) up to and including 80, then, is theoretically possible. Using a 90% rate again means that the estimated number of final outputs (service completions) for the counseling program for 1 year is 72 (80 × 0.9).

EDUCATION

The education program might define a final output (service completion) as one student completing all required course work for one semester. This approach is probably more useful than selecting a final output (service completion) on the basis of attendance, because some students can attend and not complete, whereas others may not attend 100% of the time but may still complete the required course work. Assuming the existence of curriculum requirements associated with each subject, one resident completing those requirements for each required course would constitute a final output (service completion) for the education program. Because the capacity of NBRTC is 20 residents at any one time, the maximum number of final outputs (service completions) the education program can produce in 1 year is 40 (20 residents × 2 semesters). Using a 90% rate again means that the estimated number of final outputs (service completions) for the education program for 1 year is 36 (40 × 0.9).

Exercise #4

1. Estimate the number of outputs with quality dimensions each of the three human service programs achieved last year.
2. Complete Section III: Quality, Part B, of the Annual Performance Measures Report for all three human service programs.

RESIDENTIAL CARE

Outputs with quality dimensions for the residential care program have been defined as (a) one child care day with consistency of treatment and (b) one child care day with timely resolution of exceptions. The maximum number of outputs with quality dimensions that the residential care program can produce is the same number (7,300) as the maximum number of intermediate outputs (service completions) that the program can produce. With the continued use of a 90% rate, the estimated number of outputs with quality dimensions for the residential care program for the year is 6,570 (7,300 × 0.9).

COUNSELING

Outputs with quality dimensions for the counseling program have been defined as (a) one session with the counselor of record and (b) one session beginning on time. The maximum number of outputs with quality dimensions that can be produced by the counseling program is the same number (2,080) as the maximum number of intermediate outputs (service completions) the program can produce. With the same 90% rate, the estimated number of outputs with quality dimensions for the counseling program for the year is 1,872 (2,080 × 0.9).

EDUCATION

Outputs with quality dimensions for the education program have been defined as (a) one school day with consistency of treatment and (b) one school day with all classes starting on time. The maximum number of outputs with quality dimensions that can be produced by the education program is the same number (3,600) as the maximum number of intermediate outputs (service completions) the program can produce. With the same 90% rate, the estimated number of outputs with quality dimensions for the education program for the year is 3,240 (3,600 × 0.9).

Exercise #5

1. Develop a numeric count that you believe can serve as a combined outcome performance measure for all three human service programs.
2. Estimate the number of ultimate outcomes that the residential experience achieved during the past year.
3. Complete Section IV: Outcomes, Part A, of the Annual Performance Measures Report.

COMBINED PROGRAMS

We propose developing a series of LOF scales that measure client functioning on several dimensions:

- Relationships with family members
- Social adjustment
- Emotional stability
- Educational progress
- Others

Each of the LOF scales will be scored from 1 to 5 with 1 as the lowest level of adjustment and 5 as the highest. Each client (former resident) who is rated at Level 3 or higher on all LOF scales 6 months after leaving NBRTC will be considered as having made a successful adjustment and will be considered as constituting one ultimate outcome.

We assume that on average, 10 residents leave NBRTC each year and that NBRTC has an average success rate of 80%. Thus, for the past year, eight former residents (10 former residents × 0.8) were considered successful and constituted eight ultimate outcomes.

Exercise #6

1. Complete Section V: Cost Efficiency Ratios on the Annual Performance Measures Report for all three human service programs.

RESIDENTIAL CARE

The cost per intermediate output (Section V, Part A) for the residential care program is computed by taking the total financial resources ($325,000) and dividing by the total number of intermediate outputs (7,300) the program provided. The answer is $44.52.

The number of intermediate outputs per FTE (Section V, Part B) for the residential care program is computed by taking the total number of intermediate outputs (7,300) the program provided and dividing by the total number of FTE staff (17) working in the program. The answer is 429.4.

The cost per final output (Section V, Part C) for the residential care program is computed by taking the total financial resources ($325,000) and dividing by the total number of final outputs (72) the program provided. The answer is $4,514. The number of final outputs per FTE (Section V, Part D) for the residential care program is computed by taking the total number of final outputs (72) the program provided and dividing by the total number of FTE staff (17) working in the program. The answer is 4.24.

COUNSELING

The cost per intermediate output (Section V, Part A) for the counseling program is computed by taking the total financial resources ($160,000) and dividing by the total number of intermediate outputs (2,080) the program provided. The answer is $76.92.

The number of intermediate outputs per FTE (Section V, Part B) for the counseling program is computed by taking the total number of intermediate outputs (2,080) the program provided and dividing by the total number of FTE staff (4) working in the program. The answer is 520.

The cost per final output (Section V, Part C) for the counseling program is computed by taking the total financial resources ($160,000) and dividing by the total number of final outputs (72) the program provided. The answer is $2,222.

The number of final outputs per FTE (Section V, Part D) for the counseling program is computed by taking the total number of final outputs (72) the program provided and dividing by the total number of FTE staff (4) working in the program. The answer is 18.

EDUCATION

The cost per intermediate output (Section V, Part A) for the education program is computed by taking the total financial resources ($225,000) and dividing by the total number of intermediate outputs (3,600) the program provided. The answer is $62.50.

The number of intermediate outputs per FTE (Section V, Part B) for the education program is computed by taking the total number of intermediate outputs (3,600) the program provided and dividing by the total number of FTE staff (4) working in the program. The answer is 900.

The cost per final output (Section V, Part C) for the education program is computed by taking the total financial resources ($225,000) and dividing by the total number of final outputs (36) the program provided. The answer is $6,250.

The number of final outputs per FTE (Section V, Part D) for the education program is computed by taking the total number of final outputs (36) the program provided and dividing by the total number of FTE staff (4) working in the program. The answer is 9.

Exercise #7

1. Complete Section VI: Cost Effectiveness Ratios on the Annual Performance Measures Report. *Remember,* you are using a combined numeric count ultimate outcome measure for all three human service programs.

COMBINED PROGRAMS

The cost per ultimate outcome (Section VI, Part A) is computed by taking the total financial resources ($710,000) of all three human service programs operated

TABLE B.1 Annual Performance Measures Report

	Residential Care	Counseling	Education
I. Inputs			
A. Financial resources	$325,000	$160,000	$225,000
B. Human resources	17	4	4
II. Outputs			
A. Intermediate outputs	7,300	2,080	3,600
B. Final outputs	72	72	36
III. Quality			
A. Outputs with quality dimensions	6,570	1,872	3,240
IV. Outcomes			
A. Ultimate outcomes	[	8	]
V. Cost Efficiency Ratios			
A. Cost per intermediate output	$44.52	$76.92	$62.50
B. Intermediate outputs per FTE	429.4	520	900
C. Cost per final output	$4,514	$2,222	$6,250
D. Final outputs per FTE	4.24	18	9
VI. Cost Effectiveness Ratios			
A. Cost per ultimate outcome	[	$88,750	]
B. Ultimate outcomes per FTE	[	0.32	]

by NBRTC and dividing by the total number of ultimate outcomes (8) the combined human service programs produced. The answer is $88,750.

The number of ultimate outcomes per FTE (Section VI, Part B) is computed by taking the total number of ultimate outcomes (8) the program produced and dividing by the total number of FTE staff (25) working in all three programs operated by NBRTC. The answer is 0.32.

Table B.1 provides a completed Annual Performance Measures Report.

REFERENCES

Ables, P., & Murphy, M. (1981). *Administration in the human services.* Englewood Cliffs, NJ: Prentice Hall.

Anthony, R., & Young, D. (1994). *Management control in non-profit organizations* (5th ed.). Burr Ridge, IL: Irwin.

Arizona Department of Economic Security (ADES). (1988). *Arizona taxonomy of human services.* Phoenix: Author.

Austin, M., Blum, S., & Murtaza, N. (1995). Local-state government relations and the development of public sector managed mental health care systems. *Administration and Policy in Mental Health, 22,* 203-215.

Babbie, E. (1992). *The practice of social research* (6th ed.). Belmont, CA: Wadsworth.

Benveniste, G. (1994). *The twenty-first century organization.* San Francisco: Jossey-Bass.

Boschken, H. (1994). Organizational performance and multiple constituencies. *Public Administration Review, 54,* 308-312.

Bowers, G., & Bowers, M. (1976). *The elusive unit of service.* Washington, DC: Project SHARE, Office of the Secretary, U.S. Department of Health, Education, and Welfare.

Brinkerhoff, R., & Dressler, D. (1990). *Productivity measurement: A guide for managers and evaluators.* Newbury Park, CA: Sage.

Cahill, A., & Costello, K. (n.d.). *Implementing outcomes-based performance contracting in Maine: An introduction for social service providers* [Monograph]. Orono: University of Maine, Department of Public Administration.

Carpenter, V., Ruchala, L., & Waller, J. (1991). *Service efforts and accomplishments reporting: Its time has come: Public health.* Norwalk, CT: Governmental Accounting Standards Board.

Carter, R. (1983). *The accountable agency.* Beverly Hills, CA: Sage.

Churchman, C. (1968). *The systems approach.* New York: Dell.

City of Phoenix, Arizona. (1992). *Human services department performance indicators.* Phoenix: City Auditor Department.

Connors, K. (1991). The gathering storm: Welfare in a depressed economy. *Public Welfare, 49,* 4-15.

Cornelius, D. (1994). Managed care and social work: Constructing a context and a response. *Social Work in Health Care, 20,* 47-63.

Craymer, D., & Hawkins, A. (1993). *Texas tomorrow: Strategic planning and performance budgeting.* Austin, TX: Governor's Office of Budget and Planning/Legislative Budget Office.

Cronbach, L. (1982). *Designing evaluations of educational and social programs.* San Francisco: Jossey-Bass.

Crosby, P. (1980). *Quality is free.* New York: Mentor Books.

Crosby, P. (1985). *Quality without tears: The art of hassle-free management.* New York: Plume.

Delbeck, A., Van de Ven, A., & Gustafson, D. (1975). *Group techniques for program planning.* Glenview, IL: Scott, Foresman.

Deming, W. (1986). *Out of the crisis.* Cambridge: MIT Center for Advanced Engineering Study.

Drucker, M., & Robinson, B. (1993). States' responses to budget shortfalls: Cutback management techniques. In T. Lynch & L. Martin (Eds.), *Handbook of comparative public budgeting and financial management* (pp. 189-204). New York: Marcel Dekker.

Else, J., Groze, V., Hornby, H., Mirr, R., & Wheelock, J. (1992). Performance based contracting: The case of residential treatment. *Child Welfare, 71,* 513-525.

England, M., & Goff, V. (1993). Health reform and organized systems of care. In W. Goldman & S. Fieldman (Eds.), *Managed mental health care* (pp. 5-12). San Francisco: Jossey-Bass.

Epstein, I., & Tripodi, T. (1977). *Research techniques for program planning, monitoring, and evaluation.* New York: Columbia University Press.

Epstein, P. (1992). Get ready: The time for performance measurement is finally coming! *Public Administration Review, 52,* 513-519.

Federal Accounting Standards Advisory Board (FASAB). (1994). *Managerial cost accounting standards for the federal government: Statement of recommended accounting standards, exposure draft.* Washington, DC: Author.

Federal Office of Management and Budget (FOMB). (1995). *Budget of the United States government.* Washington, DC: Government Printing Office.

Federal Quality Institute (FQI). (1990). *Criteria and scoring guidelines: The president's award for quality and productivity improvement.* Washington, DC: Author.

Feigenbaum, A. (1983). *Total quality control* (3rd ed.). New York: McGraw-Hill.

Fillenbaum, G. (1985). Screening the elderly: A brief instrumental activities of daily living measure. *Journal of the American Geriatrics Society, 33,* 698-706.

Fischer, J., & Corcoran, K. (1994). *Measures for clinical practice: Vol. 1. Couples, families, and children.* New York: Free Press.

Florida Department of Health and Rehabilitative Services (FHRS). (1986). *Assessment of the outcome measures pilot.* Tallahassee: Author.

Florida Department of Health and Rehabilitative Services (FHRS). (1995). *Performance based planning and budgeting.* Tallahassee: Author.

Fountain, J., & Robb, M. (1994). Service efforts and accomplishments measures. *Public Management, 76,* 6-12.

Franklin, C. (1982). *Gottman couples communication rating scale.* Monograph.

Gore, A. (1993). *Creating a government that works better and costs less: Report of the national performance review.* Washington, DC: Government Printing Office.

Governmental Accounting Standards Board (GASB). (1993). *Proposed statement of the Governmental Accounting Standards Board on concepts related to service efforts and accomplishments reporting.* Norwalk, CT: Author.

Governmental Accounting Standards Board (GASB). (1994). *Concepts statement no. 2 of the Governmental Accounting Standards Board on concepts related to service efforts and accomplishments reporting.* Norwalk, CT: Author.

Government Performance and Results Act, Pub. L. No. 103-62 (1993).

Hatry, H., Fountain, J., Sullivan, J., & Kremer, L. (1990). *Service efforts and accomplishments reporting: Its time has come: An overview.* Norwalk, CT: Governmental Accounting Standards Board.

Hatry, H., & Wholey, J. (Eds.). (1994). *Toward useful performance measurement: Lessons learned from initial pilot performance plans prepared under the Government Performance and Results Act.* Washington, DC: National Academy of Public Administration.

Hudson, W. (1990). *Multi-problem screening inventory.* Tempe, AZ: Walmyr.

Hudson, W. (1992). *Walmyr assessment scales scoring manual.* Tempe, AZ: Walmyr.

Juran, J. (1988). *Juran's quality control handbook* (4th ed.). New York: McGraw-Hill.

Juran, J. (1989). *Juran on leadership for quality: An executive handbook.* New York: Free Press.

Katz, S., Ford, A., & Moskowitz, R. (1963). Studies of illness in the aged: The index of ADL. *Journal of the American Medical Association, 185,* 914-919.

Kettner, P., & Martin, L. (1993). Performance, accountability and purchase of service contracting. *Administration in Social Work, 17,* 61-79.

Kettner, P., & Martin, L. (1994). Purchase of service at 20: Are we using it well? *Public Welfare, 52,* 14-20.

Kettner, P., Moroney, R., & Martin, L. (1990). *Designing and managing programs.* Newbury Park, CA: Sage.

Knapp, M. (1991). Efficiency, austerity, and economics. *Administration in Social Work, 15,* 45-63.

Kramer, R. (1994). Voluntary agencies and the contact culture: Dream or nightmare? *Social Service Review, 68,* 33-60.

Kuechler, C., Velasquez, J., & White, M. (1988). An assessment of human services program outcomes measures: Are they credible, feasible, useful? *Administration in Social Work, 12,* 71-89.

Labaw, P. (1980). *Advanced questionnaire design.* Cambridge, MA: Abt.

Leavitt, J., & Reid, W. (1981). Rapid assessment instruments for practice. *Social Work Research and Abstracts, 17,* 13-19.

Lynch, T. (1985). *Public budgeting in America* (2nd ed.). Englewood Cliffs, NJ: Prentice Hall.

Mahoney, F., & Barthel, D. (1965). Functional evaluation: The Barthel Index. *Rehabilitation, 14,* 61-65.

Martin, L. (1993). *Total quality management in human service organizations.* Newbury Park, CA: Sage.

Millar, A., Hatry, H., & Koss, M. (1977a). *Monitoring the outcomes of social services: Vol. 1. Preliminary suggestions.* Washington, DC: Urban Institute.

Millar, A., Hatry, H., & Koss, M. (1977b). *Monitoring the outcomes of social services: Vol. 2. A review of past research and test activities.* Washington, DC: Urban Institute.

Millar, R., & Millar A. (Eds.). (1981). *Developing client outcome monitoring systems.* Washington, DC: Urban Institute.

Miller, R. (1991). *Handbook of research designs and social measurement* (5th ed.). Newbury Park, CA: Sage.

Multnomah County, Oregon. (1993). *Alcohol and drug treatment: Need for a managed system.* Portland: Multnomah County Auditor.

Multnomah County, Oregon. (1994). *Multnomah County key results.* Portland: Author.

Netting, F., Kettner, P., & McMurtry, S. (1993). *Social work macro-practice.* White Plains, NY: Longman.

Nurius, P., & Hudson, W. (1993). *Human services: Practice, evaluation and computers.* Pacific Grove, CA: Brooks/Cole.

Osborn, D., & Gaebler, T. (1992). *Reinventing government.* Reading, MA: Addison-Wesley.

Palm Beach County, Florida. (1994). *Program outcome measures.* West Palm Beach: Office of Management and Budget.

Patti, R. (1987). Managing for service effectiveness in social welfare: Toward a performance model. *Administration in Social Work, 11*, 7-21.

Poertner, J., & Rapp, C. (1985). Purchase of service and accountability: Will they ever meet? *Administration in Social Work, 9*, 57-66.

Poertner, J., & Rapp, C. (1987). Moving clients center stage through the use of client outcomes. *Administration in Social Work, 11*, 23-38.

Power to the states. (1995, August 7). *Business Week*, pp. 48-56.

Pruger, R., & Miller, L. (1991). Efficiency and the social services: Part A. *Administration in Social Work, 15*, 5-24.

Rapp, C., & Poertner, J. (1992). *Social administration: A client centered approach*. White Plains, NY: Longman.

Rocheleau, B. (1988). Linking services to program goals: Two different worlds of program evaluation. *Public Administration Quarterly, 12*, 92-114.

Rosenberg, M., & Brody, R. (1974). *Systems service people*. Cleveland, OH: Case Western Reserve School of Applied Social Sciences.

Rosenbloom, D. (1995). The context of management reform. *Public Manager, 29*, 3-6.

Rossi, P., & Freeman, H. (1993). *Evaluation: A systematic approach*. Newbury Park, CA: Sage.

Schainblatt, A. (1977). *Monitoring the outcomes of state mental health treatment programs: Some initial suggestions*. Washington, DC: Urban Institute.

Spendolini, M. (1992). *The benchmarking book*. New York: AMACON.

Starling, G. (1993). *Managing the public sector* (4th ed.). Belmont, CA: Wadsworth.

Swiss, J. (1991). *Public management systems*. Englewood Cliffs, NJ: Prentice Hall.

Tatara, T. (1980). *A report of the national conference on client outcome monitoring procedures for social services*. Washington, DC: American Public Welfare Association.

Tracy, R., & Jean, E. (1993). Measuring government performance: Experimenting with service efforts and accomplishments reporting in Portland, Oregon. *Government Finance Review, 9*, 11-14.

Urban Institute. (1980). *Performance measurement*. Washington, DC: Author.

Walters, J. (1994). The benchmarking craze. *Governing, 7*, 33-37.

Walters, J. (Ed.). (1995). *Building the American community: What works, what doesn't*. Washington, DC: National Academy of Public Administration.

Wholey, J., & Hatry, H. (1992). The case for performance monitoring. *Public Administration Review, 52*, 604-610.

Wildavsky, A. (1974). *The politics of the budgetary process*. Boston: Little, Brown.

Zeithaml, V., Parasuraman, A., & Berry, L. (1990). *Delivering quality services*. New York: Free Press.

INDEX

Ables, P., 3, 32, 37
Adoption programs:
  output performance measures and, 32
  unit of service for, 40
Adult-Adolescent Parenting Inventory
  (AAPI), 80
Adult Basic Learning Education, 82
Adult day care programs:
  as example of program of services, 58
  LOF scales used to rate, 87
  outcome performance measures
  of, 60-61
Advocacy programs, unit of service for, 40
Anthony, R., 22, 23
Arizona Department of Economic Security
  (ADES), 35, 40
Arizona Taxonomy of Human Services, 35
Assertive Job-Hunting Survey (AJHS), 82
Assessment programs, unit of service for,
  40
Austin, M., 13, 14

Babbie, E., 86
Barthel, D., 75
Benchmark, definition of, 5
Benchmarking process, 106
  government programs and, 5-6
Benveniste, G., 54
Berry, L., 43
Block grants, 1
Blum, S., 13, 14

Boschken, H., 3
Bowers, G., 32, 33
Bowers, M., 32, 33
Brinkerhoff, R., 4, 7, 9, 13, 31
Brody, R., 3

Cahill, A., 109
Career Skills Assessment Program, 75, 81,
  82
Caregiver Strain Index, 83
Carpenter, V., 67
Carter, R., 2, 9, 50
Case management programs, unit of service
  for, 40
Child Abuse Potential (CAP) Inventory, 75,
  81
Child abuse prevention programs, 24
  addressing child abuse, 24
Child care services programs (AZ),
  developing unit of service for, 34
Child residential treatment center, LOF
  scales in, 92-93
Churchman, C., 4
Client end state approach:
  to developing outcome performance
  measures, 51
Client functioning, definition of, 84-85
Client outcome monitoring, 50
Client outcomes, 50
Client quality-of-life changes:
  examples of, 52

measuring, 53
Client satisfaction, 13, 19, 27, 44, 45,
    47-49, 52, 54, 61, 68
  as outcome performance measure, 96-97
  as quality performance measure, 96
  assessing, 60
  assessment of as outcome performance
    measure, 98-99
  as intermediate outcome performance
    measure, 53
  cost of, 99
  developing survey questions, 48-49
  feasibility of, 99
  precision of, 98, 99
  purpose of, 53
  reliability of, 98, 99
  selecting quality dimensions, 47, 48
  survey questionnaire, 49
  translating into numeric counts, 97
  translating quality dimensions, 47, 48
  unit cost reporting and, 99
  utility of, 98, 99
  validity of, 98, 99
Community mental health clinics:
  addressing community mental health, 24
Congregate meals programs:
  addressing poor nutrition in elderly, 20
  addressing social isolation of elderly, 20
  LOF scales for use in, 85
  performance measures for, 21
Connors, K., 1
Corcoran, K., 72
Cornelius, D., 13
Cornell Medical Index, 83
Costello, K., 109
Counseling programs, 33
  as intermediate output performance
    measure, 45
  client satisfaction survey questionnaire
    for, 49
  numeric count and, 63
  reliability of, 46, 47, 48
  responsiveness of, 46, 47, 48
  unit of service for, 33, 40
Craymer, D., 18
Crisis hotline programs, unit of service for,
    40
Crisis intervention programs, unit of
    service for, 40
Cronbach, L., 7

Crosby, P., 5, 41, 42

Day care programs:
  adult, 33, 36-37
  child, 33
Delbeck, A., 22
Deming, W., 5, 41, 42
Developmental Profile II, 75, 80
Differential Aptitude Tests, 75, 81
Disaster preparedness and relief programs,
    unit of service for, 40
Dressler, D., 4, 7, 9, 13, 31
Drucker, M., 1
Drug abuse programs:
  performance measures for different,
    25-26
  providing drug abuse counsel-
    ing/rehabilitation, 25, 26
  providing drug abuse education, 25, 26

Educational programs for underachieving
    poor children, performance measures
    for different, 29-30. See also Head
    Start
Effectiveness approach to accountability,
    3, 6-8
  examples of, 6-7
  outcomes in, 6
  outcomes to inputs ratio in, 7
  productivity and, 7
Efficiency approach to accountability,
    3, 4-5, 7
  expanded systems model and, 5
  positive reasons for, 5
  unpopularity of, 4-5
Else, J., 50, 54
Energy assistance programs, unit of service
    for, 40
England, M., 14
Environmental Standards Profile, 80
Epstein, I., 89, 92, 95
Epstein, P., 6, 14, 18

Family APGAR, 83
Family Assessment Device (FAD),
    74, 80
Family Functioning Scale, 81

Family Service Association Follow-Up
    Questionnaire, 81
Federal Accounting Standards Advisory
    Board (FASAB), 44
Federal Office of Management and Budget
    (FOMB), 12, 13
Federal Quality Institute (FQI), 44
Feedback, 3
    accountability and, 22
    definition of, 4
    efficiency perspective and, 4
Feigenbaum, A., 5, 41
Fillenbaum, G., 75
Final output performance measures, 37-40
    client focus of, 32
    See also Service completions
Final outputs, 19, 31
    client focus of, 32
Financial assistance programs, unit of
    service for, 40
Fischer, J., 72
Five-Item Instrumental Activities of Daily
    Living Screening Questionnaire, 83
Florida Department of Health and
    Rehabilitative Services (FHRS), 57,
    59, 109
    aging and adult services provided, 65, 66
    alcohol, drug, and mental health
        services provided, 65, 66
    children, youth, family services
        provided, 65, 67
    developmentally disabled persons
        services provided, 65, 67
    employment services provided, 65, 66
    numeric counts developed by, 65-67
    Service Tree approach, 57, 59
Food stamp program, 23
    unit of service for, 40
Ford, A., 75
Foster care programs, unit of service for, 40
Fountain, J., 14, 18, 67
Franklin, C., 76
Freeman, H., 3, 39, 60, 61, 86

Gaebler, T., 12
General Aptitude Test Battery, 81
Generalized Expectancy for Success Scale,
    75, 82
Goff, V., 14

Gore, A., 12
Governmental Accounting Standards Board
    (GASB), 12, 14, 15, 16, 17, 50, 55,
    61, 67
    SEA reporting initiative of, 12, 14, 104
Government Performance and Results Act
    of 1993, 11, 12, 14, 23, 56, 68, 101,
    103
    as performance measurement promoter,
        11, 12
Government programs:
    benchmarking by, 5-6
    promoting performance measurement,
        11-14
Groze, V., 50, 54
Gustafson, D., 22

Hatry, H., 7, 12, 23, 35, 50, 56, 67, 68, 101,
    103
Hawkins, A., 18
Hawthorne effect, 60
Head Start, 23
    home base, 28, 29
    in Maricopa County (Phoenix, AZ),
        27-28
    traditional, 28, 29
Home-delivered meals program, 64
    as intermediate outcome performance
        measure, 65
    as intermediate output performance
        measure, 45, 65
    as ultimate outcome performance
        measure, 65
    client satisfaction survey questionnaire
        for, 49
    numeric count and, 63
    output with quality dimension, 65
    reliability of, 46, 47, 48
    responsiveness of, 46, 47, 48
Home health aide programs, unit of service
    for, 40
Homeless shelter programs:
    addressing homelessness, 20
    performance measures and,
        0-21
    performance measures for different,
        27
    providing long-term shelter and
        comprehensive program, 27

providing short-term emergency
  shelter, 27
Home repair/adaptation/renovation
  programs, unit of service for, 40
Hornby, H., 50, 54
Hudson, W., 35, 54, 60, 72, 73, 74, 76, 77,
  79, 89
Human service program budgeting, 23
Human service program management,
  improving:
  enabling continual monitoring in, 9
  improving worker morale in, 9
  performance measurement and, 8-9
  promoting client centeredness in, 9
  providing common language in, 9
Human service program performance
  accountability, 2
  fiscal, 3
  legal, 3
  performance measurement and, 3
  process, 3
  service delivery, 3
  See also Effectiveness approach to
    accountability; Efficiency approach to
    accountability; Quality approach to
    accountability
Human service programs:
  and assumptions of social problems'
    causes, 24-29
  as units of analysis, 22-23
  crisis of confidence in, 1-2
  criteria describing, 22
  definitions of, 22
  determining number of, 22-23
  dropout rates, 37
  federal funding of, 24
  funding of, 23
  future lack of resources in, 1
  future lack of stakeholder confidence
    in, 1
  limits, 22
  multiple services of, 36
  program analysis of, 21-22
  social problems and, 20-29
  units of service catalog for, 40
  variety of, 33
  See also specific human service
    programs
Human service program stakeholders:
  accountability perspectives and, 3

categories of, 2
definition of, 2

Index of Clinical Stress (ICS), 73
Index of Family Relations, 75, 81
Index of Marital Satisfaction, Hudson's,
  72, 77
Information and referral programs, 63-64
  as intermediate outcome performance
    measure, 65
  as intermediate output performance
    measure, 45, 65
  client satisfaction survey questionnaire
    for, 49
  numeric count and, 63
  output with quality dimension, 65
  reliability of, 46, 47, 48
  responsiveness of, 46, 47, 48
  unit of service for, 33, 40
Inputs, 3, 31
  definition of, 4
  efficiency perspective and, 4
Intermediate outcome performance
  measures, 53
  as assessment of treatment effects,
    54
  definition of, 53-54
  types of, 53
Intermediate outcomes, 19
Intermediate output performance measures,
  37
  developing, 33-37, 59
  reporting, 59
  service focus of, 32
Intermediate outputs, 19, 31
  service focus of, 32
Interpreter services program,
  unit of service for, 40

Jean, E., 104, 110
Job development and placement programs,
  unit of service for, 40
Job Training Assessment Program, 81
Job Training Partnership Act program, 13,
  23
Job training programs, 33, 107-108
  addressing unemployment, 20
  performance measures for, 21

unit of service for, 40
Juran, J., 5, 41, 42

Katz, S., 75
Katz Index of Activities of Daily Living
(ADL), 82
Kettner, P., 1, 2, 3, 4, 32, 33, 37, 50, 52, 54,
60, 61, 62, 84, 108
Knapp, M., 5
Knowledge Scale, 75, 81
Koss, M., 50
Kramer, R., 1
Kremer, L., 67
Kuechler, C., 52, 54, 60, 62, 68, 84, 95, 109

Labaw, P., 86
Leavitt, J., 72
Level of functioning (LOF) scales, 19, 52,
61, 68, 70
accuracy in developing, 87
administration of to clients, 85-86
as intermediate outcome performance
measure, 53
assessing, 60
assessment of as outcome performance
measure, 94-95
as ultimate outcome performance
measure, 53
case example of, 92-93
common features of, 85
constructing, 90-92
cost of, 94, 95, 99, 100
definition of, 84
description of, 84-86
developing conceptual framework for, 86
developing descriptors for, 86-89
feasibility of, 94, 95, 99
precision of, 94, 95, 99, 100
principles of designing, 86-92
purpose of, 53
ranking of, 85
reliability of, 94, 95, 99, 100
respondent considerations in
developing, 89-90
translating into numeric counts, 94
unit cost reporting and, 94, 95, 99
used in combination, 85

using descriptive language in
constructing, 88
using descriptors to define distinctive
groupings in, 88
utility of, 94, 99
validity of, 94-95, 99, 100
Liking People Scale, 75, 82
Lynch, T., 23

Mahoney, F., 75
Managed care:
as performance measurement promoter,
12, 13-14
in California, 14
programs, 13
Managed Mental Healthcare Association
Outcomes Management Consortium,
14
Marital Communications Skills Rating
Scale, 76
Martin, L., 1, 3, 4, 6, 13, 32, 33, 37, 42, 50,
52, 54, 60, 61, 62, 84, 106, 108
Maryland Parent Attitude Survey (MPAS),
75, 80
McMurtry, S., 2
Medication/medical supplies programs,
unit of service for, 40
Millar, A., 35, 45, 50, 60, 61, 63, 68, 69
Millar, R., 35, 45, 50, 60, 61, 63, 68, 69
Miller, L., 4, 7
Miller, R., 57
Minnesota Multiphasic Personality Inven-
tory (MMPI), 74
Mirr, R., 50, 54
Modified Barthel Index of Activities of
Daily Living, 83
Moroney, R., 3, 4, 32, 37, 50, 60, 61, 62, 84
Moskowitz, R., 75
Mother and infant bonding programs,
unit of service for, 40
Multi-Problem Screening Inventory
(MPSI), 74
Multnomah County, Oregon, 57, 58, 68
Murphy, M., 3, 32, 37
Murtaza, N., 13, 14

National Academy of Public
Administration, 56

National Assessment of Education
   Progress, 81
National Performance Review:
   as performance measurement promoter,
      11, 12-13, 14
   major goal of, 12
Netting, F., 2
Numeric counts, 19, 51, 52, 61, 78
   advantages of, 70, 71
   as intermediate outcome performance
      measure, 53, 63
   as outcome performance measures of
      choice for government programs, 68,
      97
   assessing, 60
   assessment of as outcome performance
      measure, 68
   as ultimate outcome performance
      measure, 53, 63
   characteristics exclusive to, 63
   cost of, 69, 99, 100
   disadvantages of, 70, 71
   ease of use, 70
   examples of used as outcome perfor-
      mance measures, 63-65
   feasibility of, 69, 99
   interpreting ease of, 70
   precision of, 69, 70, 99, 100
   preference for, 67-68
   proposed definitions of, 62-63
   purpose of, 52, 53, 64
   reliability of, 69, 99, 100
   reporting ease of, 70
   translating client satisfaction outcomes
      into, 97
   translating LOF scales into, 94
   translating standardized measures into,
      77-78
   unit cost reporting of, 69, 99
   utility of, 69, 70, 99, 100
   validity of, 69, 70, 99, 100
Nurius, P., 35, 54, 60, 89
Nursing home care programs, unit of
   service for, 40

OARS Instrumental Activities of Daily
   Living Scale, 83
OARS Physical Health, 83

Observations, guidelines for making
   research-based, 89-90
Oregon Benchmarks:
   adult mental health programs, 58
   alcohol and drugs program, 58
   antipoverty program, 58
   as social indicator of outcome perfor-
      mance measure, 57
   children's mental health programs, 58
   downside of, 57
Oregon Options, 57
Osborn, D., 12
Outcome performance measures, 19, 20, 21
   assessing cost of, 61, 68
   assessing feasibility of, 61, 68
   assessing precision of, 61, 68
   assessing reliability of, 61, 68
   assessing unit cost reporting of, 61, 68
   assessing utility of, 60, 68
   assessing validity of, 60-61, 68
   assessment criteria for, 60-61
   assessment of four types of, 99-100
   cause-and-effect relationship and, 55-56
   definition of, 50-51
   developing through anticipated
      quality-of-life changes, 51
   for drug abuse programs, 25, 26
   for educational programs for under-
      achieving poor children, 29, 30
   for homeless shelter programs, 27, 28
   programs of services and, 58-60
   SEA reporting and, 50
   selecting, 54-55
   types of, 51-53
Outcomes, 19. See also Intermediate
   outcomes; Ultimate outcomes
Output performance measures, 19, 21
   definition of, 31
   feedback from, 31
   for drug abuse programs, 25, 26
   for educational programs for
      underachieving poor children, 29, 30
   for homeless shelter programs, 27, 28
   for human service programs, 32
   importance of, 31
   purpose of, 64
   service completions and, 39-40
   types of, 32
   using standardized measures as, 76-77

See also Final output performance
   measures; Intermediate output
   performance measures
Outputs, 3, 19, 31
   definition of, 4, 31
   efficiency perspective and, 4
   See also Final outputs; Intermediate
   outputs

Palm Beach County, Florida, 68
Parasuraman, A., 43
Parental Contact Scale, 80
Parent-Child Interaction Rating Procedure
   (P-CIRP), 80
Parenting Stress Index, 81
Parent training programs, 33
   unit of service for, 40
Patti, R., 7
Performance measurement:
   accountability perspectives of, 3, 4-8
   and improving program management,
      8-9
   and resource allocations, 8, 9-10
   and social problems-human service
      programs link, 20-29, 58
   as forced choice, 8, 10
   as management tool, 8-9
   definition of, 3
   expanded systems model and, 8
   forces promoting, 11-14
   of foster care programs, 3
   positive function of, 109-110
   reasons for adopting, 8-10
   systems model and, 3-4
Performance measurement concepts, case
      study of, 111-117
   answers to exercises, 118-124
   exercises, 113-117
Performance measurement data issues,
      106-109
   benchmarking, 106
   cost reimbursement contracting and, 108
   improving contract delivery of human
      service programs, 108-109
   improving direct delivery of human
      service programs, 106-108
   performance contracting and, 108-109
Performance measurement reporting:

for family counseling program, 106
   model format for human service
      programs, 105
Performance measurement tools, 2
Performance measures:
   data reporting issues, 103-106
   overview of, 19
   selection issues, 101-102
   *See also individual performance
      measures*
Personal escort programs, unit of service
      for, 40
Phoenix (AZ), City of, 67-68, 104, 107
Phoenix Human Resources Department, 104
Poertner, J., 9, 50
Portland (OR), City of:
   SEA reporting by, 103-104, 110
Preschool Behavior Rating Scale, 75, 80
President's Award for Quality and
      Productivity Improvement, 44
Process, 3
   definition of, 4
Program of services:
   adult day care as example of, 58
   definition of, 58
Pruger, R., 4, 7

Quality approach to accountability, 3, 5-6, 7
   expanded systems model and, 6
   ratio of outputs to inputs in, 6
   See also Total quality management
      (TQM) movement
Quality dimensions, 42
   assurance, 43
   empathy, 43
   federal government and, 44
   grafting to intermediate output
      performance measures, 45, 46-47
   most important, 43
   relating to human service programs, 45,
      46, 47
   reliability, 43
   responsiveness, 43-44
   selecting, 45, 46, 47
   tangibles, 43
Quality performance measures, 19, 21
   client satisfaction, 13, 19, 44, 45, 47-49
   for drug abuse programs, 25, 26

for homeless shelter programs, 27, 28
importance of, 41
outputs with quality dimensions, 13, 19,
    44, 45-47
purpose of, 64
types of, 44-49

Rapid assessment instruments (RAIs):
as standardized measures, 72-73
distinguishing characteristics of, 72
example of, 73
Rapp, C., 9, 50
Recreation programs, 33
Reid, W., 72
Resource allocations, performance
    measurement and, 9-10
Respite care programs, unit of service for,
    40
Robb, M., 14, 18
Robinson, B., 1
Rosenberg, M., 3
Rosenbloom, D., 12
Rossi, P., 3, 39, 60, 61, 86
Ruchala, L., 67

Schainblatt, A., 50
SEA reporting, 103
and defining outcome performance
    measures, 50
elements of, 15-18
expanded systems model and, 15
format, 19
in City of Portland, 110
local governments adopting language
    and structure of, 18
numeric counts and, 67
ratios of efforts to accomplishments
    element, 17-18
service accomplishments element, 16-17
service efforts element, 15-16
states adopting language and structure
    of, 18
using programs as unit of analysis, 22-23
SEA reporting initiative:
as performance measurement promoter,
    12, 14
in future, 14

Seattle/King County Four C's Evaluation
    Checklist for In-Home Care, Day
    Care Homes, and Day Care Centers,
    75, 80
Self-Report Family Instrument (SFI), 81
Service completions, 19, 32
and client outcomes, 39-40
case plan development approach, 38-39
definition of, 37
standardized development approach, 38
Service Efforts and Accomplishments
    (SEA) reporting initiative. See SEA
    reporting initiative
Shelter care and supervision programs, unit
    of service for, 40
Social indicator data, usefulness of, 57
Social indicators:
as ultimate outcome performance
    measures, 56-58
definition of, 56-57
experiment in use of, 57
Social problems:
child abuse/neglect, 23, 24
crime, 23, 24
drugs, 24, 25-26, 27
educational underachievement of poor
    children, 25, 27-29
homelessness, 20, 23, 25, 26-27
mental illness, 23, 24
multifaceted causes of, 24
performance measurement and human
    service programs link, 20-29, 58
poor nutrition in elderly, 20
poverty, 24
social isolation of elderly, 20
specifying, 23-24
teen pregnancy, 23
unemployment, 20, 23, 24
Social Resources Section of OARS, 83
Social Services Block Grant (SSBG), 24
Spendolini, M., 6, 106
Standardized measures, 19, 51, 52, 61, 68,
    70
achievement-focused, 74, 75
aptitude-focused, 74, 75
as intermediate outcome performance
    measure, 53
assessing, 60
assessment of as outcome performance
    measure, 78

as ultimate outcome performance
measure, 53
attitude-focused, 74, 75
behavior-focused, 74, 75
clinical cutting score in, 72
common features of, 71-72
cost of, 78, 79, 99, 100
description of, 71-73
development-focused, 74, 75
feasibility of, 78, 79, 99
for education and training, 81
for evaluating functional status, 82-83
for evaluating physical health, 83
for evaluating social status, 83
for literacy testing, 81-82
for multiple uses, 82
for social/communication skills
testing, 82
for use with families, 80-81
for use with parents and children, 80
for use with work attitudes and skills, 81
for use with young children, 80
interpersonal functioning-focused, 74, 75
intrapersonal functioning-focused, 74, 75
knowledge-focused, 74, 75
length of, 72
personality trait-focused, 74, 75
population-focused, 74, 75
precision of, 78, 79, 99, 100
problem-focused, 75
purpose of, 52-53
rapid assessment instruments (RAIs) as,
72-73
reliability of, 78, 99, 100
response scales, 76
services-focused, 74, 75
substantive focus of, 74
translating into numeric counts, 77-78
types of, 74-76
unit cost reporting and, 78, 79, 99
using as outcome performance
measures, 76
utility of, 78, 99
validity of, 78, 99, 100
who completes them, 74-75
See also specific standardized measures
Standardized measures, sources of selected:
clinical, 79
for employment-related services, 81

for services to families and children,
80-81
for services to older people, 82-83
Starling, G., 22
Sullivan, J., 67
Swiss, J., 4, 5, 6, 31
Systems model:
core elements of, 3-4
effectiveness perspective and, 7
performance measurement and, 3-4
Systems model, expanded:
efficiency perspective and, 5
performance measurement and, 8
quality perspective and, 6
SEA reporting and, 15

Tatara, T., 50, 60
Test of Adult Basic Education, 81
Total quality management (TQM)
movement:
as performance measurement promoter,
12, 13, 14
as performance measurement response,
13
definition of productivity in, 6
service quality accountability and, 5-6
Tracy, R., 104, 110
Transportation programs, unit of service
for, 40
Tripodi, T., 89, 92, 95

U.S. Department of Health and Human Services (HHS), 12, 13, 44, 57
U.S. Department of Health and Welfare, 33
U.S. Department of Housing and Urban
Development (HUD), 12, 13, 44
U.S. Department of Labor (DOL), 12, 13,
44
Ultimate outcome performance measures,
53
definition of, 54
developing, 59
reporting, 59
social indicators as, 56-58
types of, 53
Ultimate outcomes, 19
United Way of Portland (OR), 57

Units of service, 32, 45
    definition of, 33
    episode/contact, 19, 33-34, 37
    evaluation criteria, 35-36
    material, 19, 33, 34
    selection process, 35-36
    time, 19, 33, 34, 47
    types of, 33-34
Urban Institute, 3

Van de Ven, A., 22
Velasquez, J., 52, 54, 60, 62, 68, 84, 95, 109
Visiting nurse programs, unit of service for,
    40

Waller, J., 67
Walters, J., 57
Weatherization programs, unit of service
    for, 40
Wheelock, J., 50, 54
White, M., 52, 54, 60, 62, 68, 84, 95, 109
Wholey, J., 7, 12, 23, 35, 56, 68, 101, 103
Wildavsky, A., 10
WIN, 23
    training, 62

Young, D., 22, 23
Young Children's Social Desirability Scale
    (YCSD), 75, 80

Zeithaml, V., 43

ABOUT THE AUTHORS

Lawrence L. Martin is Associate Professor of Social Work and Director of the Social Administration Program at the Columbia University School of Social Work in New York City. He is the author or coauthor of 5 books and more than 40 articles dealing with human services administration, purchase of service contracting, privatization and contracting out, and state and local government. Prior to his academic career, he worked for 15 years as an administrator for state and local government agencies and nonprofit organizations.

Peter M. Kettner is Professor of Social Work at Arizona State University in Tempe. He is the author or coauthor of 5 books and more than 30 articles dealing with program planning and evaluation, purchase of service contracting, privatization, and macropractice in social work. He has served as a consultant and provided training in program planning, program evaluation, and purchase of service contracting to state and local governments and nonprofit organizations.